DIMINISHED RIGHTS

Danish lone mother families in international context

Valerie Polakow, Therese Halskov
and Per Schultz Jørgensen

The POLICY
P P
PRESS

First published in Great Britain in July 2001 by

The Policy Press
University of Bristol
34 Tyndall's Park Road
Bristol BS8 1PY
UK

Tel +44 (0)117 954 6800
Fax +44 (0)117 973 7308
E-mail tpp@bristol.ac.uk
www.policypress.org.uk

ISBN 978-1-86134-277-5

Valerie Polakow is Professor of Educational Psychology and Early Childhood Studies at Eastern Michigan University, USA. **Therese Halskov** is Associate Professor at the Danish National School of Social Work, Copenhagen. **Per Schultz Jørgensen** is former Professor of Social Psychology at the Royal Danish School of Educational Studies, Copenhagen; he served as Chairman of the Danish National Council for Children in Denmark from 1998-2001.

Cover design by Qube Design Associates, Bristol
Front cover: photograph supplied by kind permission of
www.johnbirdsall.co.uk
Printed and bound by CPI Group (UK) Ltd, Croydon, CR0 4YY

Contents

Acknowledgements

This book could not have been written without the active participation of 20 Danish lone mothers who generously shared their life stories with us over an extended period of time and we thank them warmly and appreciatively for all their time and commitment to this project. The experience for us as researchers has been moving and enlightening, and at times very disturbing. Through the mothers' stories we have learned much about policies 'on-the-ground' and have developed an inside view of vulnerability and resilience, about what is missing in terms of current policy and practice, and what lies ahead in terms of an urgent need for change.

We would also like to express our appreciation and thanks for the invaluable help provided by four organizations and institutions that put us in contact with the mothers: Boligfonden for enlige mødre og fædre, Egmontgården and two crisis centres which will remain anonymous.

Lise Thams, our research assistant for the project, has been integrally involved from the earliest stages, and has made significant contributions through her special expertise with children. She engaged in interviews with mothers, pedagogues and teachers and also conducted observations of some of the children. Cindy Guillean has provided excellent support throughout all three phases of the project: transcribing tapes, fine editing, and technical assistance, and Peggy Kahn has generously shared her time and expertise providing invaluable feedback about international policy perspectives. Valerie Polakow received a Fulbright Award to Denmark in 1995 which enabled her to begin this fruitful collaborative three-year project with Per Schultz Jørgensen and Therese Halskov. The Danish Ministry for Social Affairs financed the project through the SIBU-Fund, thus enabling us to conduct a three-year in-depth study. The Center for Research on Social Work at Den Sociale Højskole in Copenhagen promoted academic interest in the project and administered grant funds. Finally, the Robinson Fund provided funds for the preparation of the book.

The interdisciplinary and international perspectives that three different authors brought to the study have been an ongoing exciting challenge and throughout, a very rewarding collaborative partnership for all of us. We would also like to convey our appreciation to Hanne Reintoft for her interest and advice about the project and to our respective partners: Jerry Weiser (Valerie), Thomas Boje (Therese), and Ellen Schultz Jørgensen (Per) for their helpful comments, critique, and support through all the phases of the project which has resulted in two books – one Danish, one English.

An earlier version of the book *Tab af Rettigheder: Sårbare enlige mødre og deres børn* (*Loss of rights: Vulnerable lone mothers and their children*) was published in October 2000 by Hans Reitzels Publishers, Copenhagen.

ONE

Introduction: Lone motherhood in international context

"Always, always counting every penny.... The eternal and impossible choice between milk and washing soap." (Linda)

"My social worker regards me as an idiot – she does not understand anything and does not see that I develop myself.... They do not know anything about my life or my children ... and they do not ask me. So I only go to the social centre to get my social assistance, although I am really in need of talking with somebody about all my problems." (Lone)

"As a lone mother you have to be strong and dare to confront the system, otherwise you will get nothing.... Never accept a refusal in the first round!" (Hanne)

Vulnerable lone mothers embedded in the Danish social welfare system – their voices, their experiences, their life struggles – form the heart of this book as we attempt to document their daily life struggles in the context of the Danish social and political system. By presenting qualitative case studies of lone mothers and examining their narratives of experience, we develop an analysis of welfare policies and practices that is at once localized, and embedded in a specific Danish context, yet reaches beyond with implications for both Europe and the United States.

Lone mothers and their children have historically been constituted as a 'problem' constituency – variously demonized, stigmatized, and marginalized. While lone mothers have fared better in countries such as Denmark, where universal family support policies are present, their lives nevertheless are qualitatively 'less than' their fellow citizens, and our study investigates both why and how. For if pulling up the blinds on Danish universalism reveals bleak and grim family worlds for many vulnerable lone mothers, what lessons can be learnt by other countries contemplating or implementing welfare reforms?

Lone parenthood, and specifically lone motherhood, has taken very different pathways in Europe, Britain, and the US, and many feminist social policy analysts have argued that single motherhood is a litmus test of gendered social rights (Hobson, 1994). While welfare state regimes differ markedly from the 'residual' in the US to the universal in Scandinavia, there are strikingly similar cross-national problems and obstacles confronting vulnerable low-income single mothers with children: lack of access to education and to stable self-sufficient employment, caregiving restrictions related to time and health resources, and a family life frequently destabilized by violent husbands and partners. In the European Union (EU) 36% of lone parent families (predominantly lone mothers) live below the poverty line, compared to 17% of all families in the EU (Eurostat, 1997); and in fact whatever poverty measure is used, lone-mother families emerge as one of the poorest groups (Roll, 1992).

In Britain lone-mother families are characterized by poverty and their dependency on state benefits, with over 50% dependent on income support for the bulk of their income (Duncan and Edwards, 1997a), and in the US[1] the poverty rate for lone mothers with children under 18 is 35.7% (US Census Bureau, 2000a). In Scandinavia, despite progressive universal policies, demographic statistics and surveys convey a picture of gender segregation in the labour market where women are concentrated in specific occupations with lower pay, lower status, and less secure jobs, and these trends are exacerbated for single mothers with young children. In both Denmark and Sweden the employment situation of lone mothers has deteriorated significantly since the 1980s, and they are excluded from the labour market to a far greater extent than mothers in two-parent families (Larsen and Sørensen, 1994; Björnberg, 1997). Extensive studies of poverty conducted in the mid-1980s based on minimum budgets documented that the largest group living in poverty were lone mothers (Hansen, 1989). The mean figure for 29-79 year olds was 4% but for lone mothers it was 18%. These results have been confirmed by subsequent surveys conducted during the late 1990s (Alsted Research, 1998; Pedersen and Smith, 1999).

As we see in this qualitative study of women's lives in Denmark, single mothers occupy a specific gendered space and readily fall through the ever-widening holes of a universalistic society which has failed to recognize the specific life-world obstacles of such families. However, in contrast to Denmark, where vulnerable lone mothers live diminished and marginalized lives, vulnerable lone mothers in the US encounter a dramatically different set of life circumstances: widespread destitution, homelessness, and hunger, where 25.8% of the children in female-headed households live below 50% of the federal poverty line, that is, with incomes below $6,401 per year (Children's Defense Fund, 1999). Overall, 20% of children under the age of 18 live in poverty, the numbers increasing proportionate to age, so that the poorest citizens are also the youngest, with 27% of children under three living in poverty. Hence it is clear the policy implications of the feminization of poverty must also be understood in terms of a family survival continuum, and what it means to be poor in Denmark is qualitatively different from chronic destitution in the US. However, in both contexts single mothers and their children suffer damaging consequences, and while lives are ravaged at one end of the continuum, at the other end, they are nevertheless diminished and impaired when social citizenship rights fail to take account of the unique position of lone-mother families. In this chapter Scandinavian, UK, and US discourses and policies will briefly be examined in order to situate our life-world study in a broader international context.

Contrasting discourses about lone motherhood

In Scandinavia, a pragmatic 'equality'-oriented approach has shaped the discourse about lone motherhood so that *parenting* is stressed rather than *marital status*, and social and family policies have focused on promoting equality in the living conditions of children irrespective of family form. Scandinavian welfare states have generally been evaluated as 'woman-friendly' (Hernes, 1987; Siim, 1997), with strong universal policies that provide social insurance, universal child care and health care, advance child maintenance support, and child, family and lone parent allowances designed to insure the equality status of lone parents (Larsen and Sørensen, 1994; Björnberg, 1997). Siim argues that since the 1970s the Danish welfare state has shifted from a male breadwinner to a dual-breadwinner model, so that for all mothers the labour market plays a central role, and lone mothers are perceived as no different from other mothers, thereby equalizing the status of all mothers. Hence "the cultural image of lone mothers has changed from that of a weak and dependent group to a strong and autonomous group ... lone mothers have not been either an ideological or a political problem during the last 25 years" (Siim, 1997, pp 142-3). Similarly Björnberg (1997) argues that lone parenthood in Sweden has become an accepted social phenomenon and that open stigmatization of lone parenthood or lone motherhood is rare. The academic discourse about 'lone mothers' has also been scrutinized in terms of the appropriate use of a civil administrative category such as 'lone mother' to designate a group of people, who experience structural constraints and social pressures very much like the marginalized situations of other vulnerable groups (immigrants in general, young unemployed people, lonely elderly people). The category 'lone mother', it has been argued, promotes stereotypes about women living alone with their children, and frames them as mothers who are overburdened with personal problems and unable to handle their own or their children's lives (Scheffer-Kumpala, 1997).

However, a neutral discourse about lone parenthood which discards the distinctive differences and discrimination that solo mothers experience, may also serve to mask the specific gendered institutional practices that locate lone mothers, particularly those who begin poor and have little or no education, in a marginalized space where labour market discrimination, family violence, and the burdens of caring alone for young children clearly take their toll. Mothers who lack a 'dual' breadwinner partner also lack back-up support when their children are sick, their time and material resources are scarce, and crisis situations such as chronic illness impact their capacity to maintain a viable attachment to the labour force. It is also clear that in Scandinavia, as elsewhere, there are two distinct categories of lone mothers – those who are well educated and economically self-sufficient with the resources and networks to obtain care-giving assistance when needed; and low-income lone mothers who have little or no education, who are also job-poor and primarily dependent on secondary public transfers for daily living, and, lacking strong social networks, exist on the margins of society.

The marginalized lone mothers portrayed in our study are increasingly becoming part of an emerging postmodern underclass in Scandinavia, experiencing new forms of stigmatization based on social class, ethnicity, and their vulnerable status as state-dependent lone mothers. Such categories of lone mothers do not fit the gender-blind welfare state analyses of leading social policy researchers such as Esping-Andersen (1990), who has characterized social citizenship rights in welfare states by their degree of decommodification – because the Swedish 'supported workers who mother' model (Björnberg, 1997), and the Danish 'dual bread-winner norm' (Siim, 1997) mean that lone mothers, like all parents, are expected to provide for themselves and their children by combining wage work, family entitlements, and social services. In Denmark lone mothers who do not 'make it' in this 'equality' system are clearly viewed as social problems despite the fact that gendered institutional structures and practices act as barriers to their integration. Furthermore, domestic violence and its impact has not been adequately examined by social policy researchers as a severe structural constraint – and when wages from work are low, suitable housing is scarce and often unavailable, access to vocational and post-secondary educational opportunities are restricted, and social support services in the public system are diminished, a significant number of lone mothers and their children are constructed as 'social problems'. However, despite the above imaging of lone mothers, the Scandinavian discourse about lone motherhood has not been tainted by the punitive 'immorality' and 'social threat' discourses so pervasive in the United States and Britain.

Lone mothers and the 'social threat' discourse in the United States

In the United States during the 1990s when President Clinton pledged to "end welfare as we know it", the Democrats became, for the first time, complicit partners in a decades-long Republican assault on lone mothers. The discourse of single motherhood in the US, historically anchored in a rhetoric of immorality deeply embedded in racial and gendered inequality, and punitive policies towards the poor, has emerged as a racially coded pæon to work and 'personal responsibility', where poverty is viewed as an individual/family pathology – a behavioural disorder and the product of bad personal choices. As Schram (1995) points out, public policies that are designed to distinguish the 'worthy' that work, from the 'unworthy' on welfare, create a discourse that,

> ... re-creates the ugly reality of a poverty based on neglect and indifference that discourages extension of aid to families whose heads do not have paid jobs, in particular mothers with children and this invidious distinction reinforces a bifurcated welfare state that divides along gender, race, and class lines, with women and minorities often being relegated to programs with inferior benefits. (Schram, 1995, p 177)

Charles Murray, an influential right-wing policy analyst, argued in the *Wall Street Journal* in the early 1990s that the state should "end all economic support for single mothers.... From society's perspective to have a baby that you cannot care for yourself is profoundly irresponsible and the government will no longer subsidize it" (Murray, 1993). In 1996 the Republican-controlled Congress passed, and President Clinton signed, the most far-reaching piece of social policy legislation in five decades, dismantling the federal entitlement to public assistance for all poor single mothers and their children. Under the new law, the Personal Responsibility and Work Opportunity Reconciliation Act (PL 104-193), which President Clinton signed into law on 22 August 1996, Title 1VA of the 1935 Social Security Act was repealed and replaced by state-administered block grants, where public assistance to poor children and their single parents was made conditional on meeting mandatory work requirements. Known as TANF (temporary assistance to needy families), such 'welfare' was time-limited to five years. Strict penalties, culminating in a complete cut-off of benefits to the family, were enforced for non-compliance with the mandatory work requirements. Despite the chronic unavailability of licensed subsidized infant and preschool care in most states, federal law mandated that all single mothers with babies of a year old had to meet mandatory work requirements; and in some states such as New York, Michigan, Wisconsin, and Massachusetts, this requirement was increased to coerce mothers with babies over 12 weeks into mandatory work requirements as a condition of receiving benefits. The ensuing results have wreaked havoc on lone-mother families. As more and more families are pushed off welfare into the low-wage work force, 71% of workers earn below the federal poverty line, and lone mothers in short-term low-wage employment face multiple child care obstacles and developmentally dangerous child care (Kahn and Polakow, 2000), with the number of destitute children growing by half a million since welfare 'reforms' were instituted (Sherman et al, 1998).

During the Congressional debates leading up to 'welfare reform', single mothers were publicly denounced in Congress and demonized on national television as "breeding mules", "alligators", and as "monkeys" (Polakow, 1997). Representative Clay Shaw, Jr, who shepherded welfare legislation through the House, stated, "it may be like hitting a mule with a two by four but you've got to get their attention" (DeParle, 1994). When the Welfare Bill reached the Senate, Senator Phil Gramm demanded, "We've got to get a provision that denies more and more cash benefits to women who have more and more babies while on welfare" (Toner, 1995). Hence during the 1990s both the Republican Congress and a Democratic Administration under President Clinton "brought welfare to the centre of the political stage in order to point to poor women, especially minority women, as the source of America's troubles. Welfare and the women who depend on it have been cast as the locus of a kind of moral rot..." (Piven, 1995, p xiii).

This public assault on single mothers in the US took place against a backdrop of increasing poverty, destitution, and homelessness for the poorest Americans and effectively illustrates the dire policy consequences of the social threat discourse. During the 1990s, as welfare was being dismantled, single mothers comprised 70-90% of homeless families nationwide (Bassuk, 1990; Steinbock, 1995; Bassuk et al, 1996). Over 50% of homeless families became homeless because the mother fled domestic violence (National Clearinghouse for the Defense of Battered Women, 1994); and one in four homeless persons was a child younger than the age of 18 (National Coalition for the Homeless, 1996). Furthermore, reports from the Food and Research Action Center indicated that four million children under the age of 12 went hungry during part of each month, and that during the 1990s there were over 13 million children without health insurance (Children's Defense Fund, 1998). Despite the record of the US in failing to develop social insurance policies that provide for the basic health, shelter, and daily living needs of its most vulnerable citizens – poor women and children – female and child poverty was cast as a 'moral' problem, tied to public rhetoric about 'family values' and 'family breakdown' which, in turn, was used to rationalize the demise of 'welfare as we knew it'.

The term 'feminization of poverty' has been widely used to describe the particular plight of single mothers in the US who experience occupational segregation and workplace discrimination, occupy part-time service sector jobs with little or no benefits, and retain primary care of children. As single mothers, they are disproportionately poor and face an alarming array of obstacles which threaten their family stability (Pearce, 1978; Ehrenreich and Piven, 1984; Goldberg and Kremen, 1990; Gordon, 1990; Polakow, 1993; Kahn and Polakow, 2000). Unmet needs in housing, health care, and child care have coalesced to form a triple crisis where single mothers, as both providers and nurturers of their children, cannot sustain family viability when they are low-wage earners, with no family support provisions in place to act as a buffer against the ravages of the market economy, where full-time work at minimum wage keeps them below the poverty line. There is no national health care system and no universal family support policies such as paid maternity/parental leave, national child/family allowances, or a national subsidized child care system for infants and preschool children (Kamerman and Kahn, 1991, 1995; Polakow, 1993). Headstart, the public early childhood intervention program for poor children, developed during the 1960s 'war on poverty', provided access to only 36% of income eligible children during 1998 (Children's Defense Fund, 1999). The child care crisis compounds the situation with many low-wage mothers unable to afford the high costs of private child care, and there is an acute national crisis of licensed, affordable child care. Recent national reports have documented widespread problems in many states: unsafe, unsanitary centres, poor quality care, lack of regulation, chronic unavailability of infant care, and closed access to low-income families (US General Accounting Office, 1993; Ebb, 1994; Helburn, 1995; Children's Defense Fund, 1996, 2000).

While social security for elderly Americans is still considered an earned entitlement, social security for children (who in turn must depend on their parents' benefits) forms part of a completely different discourse in the US, because the parents, specifically poor mothers of dependent children, are viewed as undeserving of government support.

The anti-welfare and 'underclass' punitive discourses that have targeted lone mothers and pregnant teenagers have promoted a continuing public perception of poverty as a private individual problem, with little or no reference to structural obstacles and restraints: the low-wage labour market, inaccessible housing and child care, racial and gender discrimination, and the absence of social insurance policies.

Lone mothers and the 'social threat' discourse in Britain

In 1998, New Labour's publication of the Green Paper *A new contract for welfare* (DSS, 1998) proposed to rebuild welfare around work, and its provisions bore a striking resemblance to the Personal Responsibility and Work Opportunity Reconciliation Act (PL 104-193) in the US, extolling the values of work and attempting to push more lone parents into low-wage work, emphasizing the costs of welfare fraud and blaming the 'underclass' and a culture of dependency for poverty and exclusion. However, as Stepney, Lynch and Jordan point out, while the Blair government has followed the lead of the US rather than Europe in fashioning the New Deal, such policy prescriptions "follow a long conservative cultural tradition in Britain. Poverty has been reified as a subject of moral weakness, panic, or fear" (Stepney et al, 1999, p 119). During the 1990s Charles Murray and fellow right-wing policy analysts such as Lawrence Mead and James Q. Wilson gained prominence in Britain – in both Conservative and New Labour circles. Frequently cited in *The Sunday Times*, and by the right-wing Institute of Economic Affairs, Murray's moral panic exhortations and prescriptions for patriarchal nuclear families, marriage, and the return to traditional family values, found strong support not only among Thatcher hardliners and Tory traditionalists, but among many Liberals as well (Roseneil and Mann, 1996). The social costs of lone motherhood and the support for such 'promiscuity' were cited as leading to moral disintegration directly attributed to the benefits of the welfare state.

The cross-national discourse parallels are striking, as in both Britain and the US, lone mothers were identified as a large and growing group who are disproportionately dependent on welfare. The findings from the Bristol Poverty Line Survey (cited in Stepney et al, 1999) indicate that over a third of lone parents are living in "absolute poverty" (p 118). Despite Tony Blair's recently declared war on child poverty, Britain fares only marginally better than the US in terms of appalling rates of child poverty, according to the recent UNICEF 2000 Report which lists Britain 20th in 23 countries studied, barely ahead of the US, but trailing Turkey and Greece (*The Economist*, 17 June 2000, 'Britain: More bad news', vol 355, p 57). The confluence of child poverty and the lack of adequate social insurance policies for lone-mother families has not led to any attempt to institutionalize a sound and supportive family policy nor to assess the overall impact of welfare policies affecting lone parents but rather to a strident moral crusade that inveighs against dependency and promotes "the imperatives of the new, 'flexible' labour market, with its attendant insecurities and exploitations" (Stepney et al, 1999, p 121).

In 1996, Yvette Cooper, writing for the *New Statesman* in an article entitled 'Me Blair, you Clinton', argued that "a single mother whose benefit runs out in the US will have plenty of responsibilities but very few rights", but doubted whether "the US welfare bill really could be a precursor to a Labour-led assault on the welfare state here". Yet the 1990s rhetoric in Britain bore striking parallels to the demonization of lone mothers and the moral panic about a 'dependency culture' in the US. As Lewis points out, "During the early 1990s, political and media commentary on lone mothers became extremely vicious.... Nowhere else in Europe have lone mothers attracted such a negative press" (Lewis, 1998, p 7). In 1992, at the Conservative Party Conference, Social Security Secretary Peter Lilley declared that he intended to "close down the something-for-nothing society", and this was followed by an attack on teenage girls for becoming pregnant "just to jump the housing list" (Sinfield, 1994, pp 130-1). In 1993 *The Sunday Times* had a special pull-out section entitled 'Wedded to Welfare; Do they want to marry a man or the state?' (Roseneil and Mann, 1996), and Charles Murray was again lavishly quoted. Hence the 'underclass–immorality–illegitimacy' triage so common in the US also became well entrenched in Britain as the image of the lone mother predator preying on the generosity of taxpayers was promoted.

As in the US, the social threat discourse in Britain took place in a society where poverty was becoming increasingly feminized. Twenty per cent of families are now headed by a lone parent in Britain, of which over 90% are lone-mother families – the highest rate in the EU – and most are economically marginal, with over 60% having incomes less than half the national average (Duncan and Edwards, 1997a). Women as workers predominantly occupy low-wage clerical and service sector jobs, concentrated in a narrow economic band where pension rights and other benefits are less or non-existent. Women suffer employment discrimination in terms of wages, promotion and security, and two thirds of women with dependent children who work part time do so for less than 31 hours a week; hence they experience further discrimination in terms of employment rights, pensions, and training (Proceedings of the House of Commons Employment Committee, 1995). There has been a general erosion of entitlement to income supports for lone mothers under the 'personal responsibility' rhetoric and transplanted workfare policies from the US which have been institutionalized in the New Deal for Lone Parents as of October 1998 ('New Deal', www.dfee.gov.uk), and which require parents with school-age children to attend interviews with employment advisors as part of an overall strategy to reduce dependence on income support. But overall reductions in lone parents' benefits and the lone parent premium since 1998 ('Income Support – General Information [2000]', www.dss.gov.uk) leaves lone mothers substantially worse off if they are employed in low-wage part-time work and receiving Family Credit subsidies. Hence lone mothers, argue Guttenplan and Margaronis, have been caught in the New Deal of 1998, which "failed miserably because few women chose to leave their children in badly organized day care so they could stack shelves in the local Safeway"(Guttenplan and Margaronis, 2000, p 23).

While Britain has the highest number of lone-parent families in the EU, they are far less likely to be in full-time employment, because Britain ranks among the worst in Europe for day care provision, and has adopted a 'hands-off approach' to the crisis of day care, playing no direct role in promoting a national system of public day care nor in stressing the significance and benefits of early day care for children in contrast to other European countries (Duncan and Edwards, 1999). Britain's lack of commitment to universal day care has been characterized as lacking a commitment to equality as outlined by the European Community (EC) legislation with its guiding principles of equal treatment. While Britain ratified the UN Convention on the Rights of the Child in 1989 (unlike the US which still remains a pariah nation together with Somalia in failing to ratify) it has ignored Article 18, which gives children of working parents the right to day care (Edwards and Mckie, 1993/94). The Under Fives Initiative launched in the 1990s was short-lived, terminating targeted funds for the children of lone mothers after only three years, leading Edwards and Mckie to argue that "such bursts of short-term money hardly contribute towards [a] coherent child care policy" (1993/94, p 48). During the 1990s Britain also had one of the lowest number of child care places in the EU and, more significantly, the lowest public provision – 90% of child care was unsubsidized. For infants and toddlers under three it was even worse, dropping to a dismal 2%! (Edwards and Mckie, 1993/94; Proceedings of the House of Commons Employment Committee, 1995). Hence substantial numbers of lone mothers with young children have been unable to take up paid employment because lack of access to child care constitutes a major barrier (Bradshaw and Millar, 1991; Duncan and Edwards, 1997b).

The controversial 1991 Child Support Act, which received a great deal of 'feckless father' hype mirroring the 'dead-beat dad' rhetoric in the US, has similarly been of little help to low-income solo mothers as, "in most cases it is not mothers and children who benefit from the increase in maintenance payments, but the Treasury" (Lister, 1994, p 218). As in the US an increased emphasis on collection of child support has paralleled the cuts to lone mothers and child benefits, rationalized by the 'personal responsibility' rhetoric so that in both societies, unmarried and solo mothers are stigmatized as costly social threats (Roseneil and Mann, 1996; Duncan and Edwards, 1997a; Polakow, 1997).

In societies where lone mothers and their children are not only stigmatized, but blamed for their poverty, the stigma is far more damaging, and a discourse of dependency quickly shifts the ground from a structural analysis of poverty to psychological and cultural deficits – a retreat from public responsibility by the state to serve as the primary agency of social insurance. When such discourses result in radical policy reversals, such as we see in the welfare legislation of 1996 in the United States, the consequences lead to widespread violations of rights. Mink argues that in the United States, "The Personal Responsibility Act removes single mothers from the welfare state to a police state" (Mink, 1998, p 133), denying them fundamental family rights as "welfare law now forbids mothers who remain single to work inside the home caring for [their own] children" (p 30).

If single motherhood is 'a litmus test' of gendered social rights, single mothers and their children in Britain and the United States have experienced a steady erosion of rights under postmodern third wave 'New Democrat' and 'New Labour' governments, which have continued the legacy of their respective Conservative predecessors. The United States is clearly the most extreme example of the violation of social and family rights, and both the discourse and policies serve as ominous foreshadowing to a new millennium of globalization and privatization as global capitalism takes its toll on domestic infrastructures, exporting jobs, downsizing, non-unionized contract workers and the inexorable reduction of public entitlements and social citizenship rights.

Danish lone mothers

Hence, viewed from the vantage point of a cross-national lens, Danish lone mothers still retain fundamental social citizenship rights, and the lone mothers in our study undeniably live qualitatively better lives than do their counterparts in the United States or Britain. However, the comparison point should not be to the lowest common denominator, currently exemplified by the new welfare policies in the United States and Britain. Despite existing social insurance policies, the lives of Danish lone mothers in our study are riddled with multiple problems and even more troubling, decreasing social supports.

In Denmark, about 20% of all families with children under 18 years are headed by one parent, and almost 90% of these families are lone-mother households. Lone-mother families still constitute one of the poorest groups in the country (Smith and Naur, 1998), and one third of lone mothers receive social assistance for some period of every year. Despite a progressive welfare state system in Denmark with a strong safety net in terms of public day care, universal health care, and higher education, there are certain recurrent problems that appear to strike particularly vulnerable groups of lone mothers and young children. Lone mothers have higher rates of unemployment, spend a longer time on social assistance, and have greater difficulty escaping the poverty trap In addition, the distance between the principles embodied in the former and the new Danish Social Assistance laws[2], and the implementation of such laws, appear to vary from municipality to municipality, which in turn is tied to policies of decentralization and localization creating differential access to forms of social support available to lone mothers and their children.

These factors raise important concerns about key principles of the Danish welfare state: universalism and social equality. While many in Danish society continue to experience economic prosperity, poverty continues to increase among lone mothers. How poor can the state allow specific groups to become before revisiting the gaps of universalism? The way in which lone mothers experience the public welfare system, and how that system is interpreted and administered, is an area that requires critical appraisal.

A brief overview of the research study

In order to portray the existential realities of lone-mother families in poverty, we chose a qualitative case study approach to look inside the windows of vulnerable Danish families. Our research approach emphasizes the importance of local knowledge, and, with Clifford Geertz, we share the belief that "small facts speak to large issues" (Geertz, 1973, p 23); that a detailed microanalysis may lead to fruitful social policy development. With this goal in mind and with the express permission and collaboration of the lone mothers who volunteered to participate in the study, we tell their stories and use their narratives to illuminate critical problems within the public welfare system and analyse the broader social policy implications. In the telling of such stories, we attempt to honour the struggles and resilience of both the women and their children, and to keep their voices at the centre of our policy and practice analysis and recommendations.

Research approach: methodology, research participants, and research setting

The study initially investigated the life situations of 20 lone mothers and their children using an interdisciplinary approach, drawing from theoretical perspectives in anthropology, sociology, psychology and social work. We interviewed 20 lone mothers, most of them three times, over a two-year period from 1996 to 1998. The interviews were open-ended and, as Scheper-Hughes (1992) describes, "more dialogic than monologic", creating richly textured data. The interviews were analysed as narrative accounts that lodge particular themes in place, time, and social context (Geertz, 1973; Coles and Coles, 1989; Denzin and Lincoln, 1998). In order to understand the 'gestalt' and life-world reality of the families, we also observed the mothers and children in their homes, and visited the day care centres and schools that some of the children attended. The detailed case studies that we developed from the interviews and ethnographic observations follow in the tradition of qualitative case studies that focus on the lives of low-income families (Stack, 1974, 1996; Abraham, 1993; Polakow, 1993; Halskov, 1994).

In the first phase of the study, the primary focus was on listening to and audio-taping the mothers' stories. In phase two the study was extended to focus intensively on eight of the children from the sample of 20 lone-mother families. With the mothers' permission, the children were interviewed and/or observed at home, in day care centres and in schools. In addition, day care pedagogues, teachers, and other significant adults in the children's lives were interviewed. Mothers were also invited to participate in these interviews and all wanted to do so. The 20 mothers and their children were all residents in Copenhagen or the environs. The age of the mothers varied from 21 to 38 years old, each with one to three children under the age of 14. Six of the mothers were immigrants. The children participating in phase two of the study were all boys. This was not a specific study focus, but rather resulted from a confluence of factors: more boys in the study sample, mothers' anxieties about their sons, and the selection of families for phase two. (For more detailed profiles of the mothers and children, see Appendix A.)

Our contact with the 20 mothers was established through four organizations: Boligfonden for enlige mødre og fædre (The Housing Foundation for Single Mothers and Fathers), a homeless crisis centre for women and men, a crisis centre for women, and Egmontgården, a lone-mother facility which was formerly private but is now run by Copenhagen municipality[3]. We asked the organizations about possible contacts with lone mothers who had been in contact with the public social system for long periods and who had been struggling with multiple barriers and constraints. Almost all the lone mothers identified by the organizations agreed to be interviewed, and all lone mothers with whom we met generously agreed to participate in our project. Their willingness to participate in the project and their openness and trust were, to a large degree, mediated by their desire to tell their stories in accordance with a basic principle of the study: giving visibility and paying heed to the mothers' voices and stories, their experiences, and their perceptions of the institutions they encountered (day care centres, schools, and social welfare centres) – consequently this documentation forms the core narrative evidence of the study.

Throughout the project we have attempted to empower and advocate for the mothers and their children. Perhaps the stories about these families would have been framed differently if we had also interviewed their social workers at the social welfare centres or denied the mothers access to the interviews with their children's pedagogues and teachers. However, we chose to give the principal voice to lone mothers who, in this period of their lives, are extremely dependent on the welfare system. For we believe that the reality of the social welfare system is best reflected in the experiences of those who need it most.

The organization of the book

In *Diminished rights* we present the life stories of 14 mothers and their children. For a number of reasons, including confidentiality and the need to honour the wishes of some mothers, 6 of the 20 do not appear in the book, but many of their experiences are mirrored in the words of those who do tell their stories. Part I, *Whither equality? The worlds of Danish lone mothers*, presents case studies of six mothers struggling to overcome critical obstacles in their lives and that of their children: poverty, unemployment/low-wage employment, lack of access to post-secondary education, lack of access to housing, and chronically sick children – all the structural and systemic barriers that serve to marginalize and stigmatize. While the mothers' particular situations are embedded in a unique time and space, their stories reach beyond themselves and envelop many other lives of solo mothers whose stories are not told here. In Part II, *The outsiders – the worlds of ethnic minority lone mothers*, a detailed case study of one lone mother and her son is presented, followed by shorter portraits of five additional lone mothers. Their stories serve to illuminate the phenomenon of *otherness* as their experiences are discussed in terms of their dual outsider status – as both ethnic minorities and low-income solo mothers. Part III, *Violence and the culture of silence*, portrays the family worlds of two Danish lone mothers who have been repeatedly terrorized by violent men. The disturbing prevalence of domestic violence in the lives of many lone mothers and their children is analysed, as are the questions of child custody and the legal rights of lone mothers. The final chapter, *Policy and practice recommendations*, summarizes the major obstacles facing lone mothers in Denmark and raises questions of equality, universalism, and social citizenship rights in a broader international context; and concludes with a set of recommendations for changes in social welfare policies and practices in Denmark.

Notes

[1] The poverty line in the EU is defined as half the median household income and is adjusted for family size. In the US a much lower poverty threshold is used, based on the Orshansky Index of 1965. The poverty threshold for the US for a family of four was $17,029 in 1999, but the median household income for a family of four was $59,768. If the US were to use the common European formula, millions more families would be classified as living in poverty (US Census Bureau, 2000b).

[2] The Act on Active Social Policy (*Lov om Aktiv Socialpolitik*) was put into force in 1998. The law is one of three laws that replaced the Act on Social Assistance from 1976 (*Lov om Social Bistand*). The Act on Active Social Policy (*Lov om Aktiv Socialpolitik*) relates to economic, labour, and educational issues that affect lone mothers. The Act requires a person to demonstrate activity in the labour market by participation in work activation programmes in order to gain access to social assistance. Working capacity must be evaluated before rehabilitation activities can be granted (Part 6, §46, Act on Active Social Policy). There must be demonstrable proof that one's working capacity is circumscribed due to physical, psychological or social reasons.

However, the Act on Active Social Policy is a framework designed to guide local decisions, creating possibilities at the local municipal level for very different interpretations about the meaning of 'limited capacity for work'.

The former law of 1976, the Act on Social Assistance (*Lov om Social Bistand*), also included some work requirements as a condition for receiving social assistance. But the terms were far more vaguely formulated. Access to rehabilitation (*revalidering*) support through §43 in the Act on Social Assistance was not only related to working capacity, but also included the possibility of giving 'rehabilitation support' (often for social reasons to support lone mothers) – if these education activities could improve a person's capability to provide for oneself in the future. It was not necessary to evaluate a person's working capacity before starting rehabilitation.

While local interpretation and implementation of §43 in the Act on Social Assistance had resulted in restrictions during the last decade, there is no doubt that the new 1998 law, Act on Active Social Policy will, with its sharp focus on immediate work requirements, severely reduce the possibilities for lone mothers to receive educational support for more long-term and consistent educational activities.

It should be noted, however, that contrary to the US, where mandatory work requirements coerce lone mothers into work when their infants are 12 months (and in some states, such as Michigan, Wisconsin, Massachusetts and New York, only 12 weeks), without provision for affordable and quality day care, Danish lone mothers are not required to work unless they have day care placements for their children and then only after their paid maternity leave is completed (26 weeks), which may be extended to 52 weeks.

[3] Boligfonden for enlige mødre og fædre (the Housing Foundation for Single Mothers and Fathers) is a private organization which owns and runs a few properties, among them a communal house/college for lone parents pursuing education. The organization offers counselling on housing, economic and educational problems. It makes small cash grants for emergencies and relocation expenses and subsidizes recreational activities and holidays for the lone parents receiving organizational assistance.

Egmontgården is a housing facility for lone parents that was initially built as a private foundation but is now run by Copenhagen municipality. It serves lone parents with housing and other social or personal problems. There are 102 small low-rent flats where lone parents (almost all mothers) live temporarily with their young children under seven years. The average stay is about eight months. Comprehensive services are provided to residents by staff social workers and health visitors (visiting paediatric nurses).

Part I:
Whither equality? The worlds of Danish lone mothers

Lone motherhood and the struggle to survive

The lives of vulnerable lone mothers in Denmark clearly belie the myths of equality in terms of education, unemployment and poverty. Tightly stretched penny-pinching budgets, lack of access to good quality housing, and diminished rights to an education all characterize the daily lives of the lone mothers in this study. Lacking such vital components of a stable existence, the quality of life for lone mothers and their children is impaired, severely disrupting the physical and psychological health of the family, and eroding the capacity to build sustainable relationships, create support networks, and provide one's children with the basic necessities for a stable and nurturing home.

How does coping with a chronic lack of resources and confronting a myriad of critical daily obstacles shape the lives of lone mothers and their children? This question forms a continuing thread throughout the book as we seek to portray the life-worlds not only of lone mothers, but of their children as well; so that the 'ecology' of each family (Bronfenbrenner, 1995) is understood as a complex and multi-layered system. By listening to the voices of lone mothers we learn first-hand about the 'nuts and bolts' of daily survival – of lives lived on the bottom rung of a ladder strewn with hurdles that block easy ascent.

TWO

Critical obstacles confronting lone mothers

The impact of poverty

Many studies of lone-mother families have traditionally focused on the psychological aspects of lone motherhood and the relationships between mothers and their children (Ross and Sawhill, 1975; Hetherington, 1999), as well as the impact of 'fatherless' families and the effects in particular on young boys raised without the presence of a father in their daily lives (Lamb, 1986; Hurstel, 1993; Jalmert, 1993). However, scant attention has been paid to the existential impact of material poverty in which an increasing number of lone mothers and their children live (Ingerslev et al, 1992; Polakow, 1993; Larsen and Sørensen, 1994; Alsted Research, 1998). Findings from the Danish National Institute of Social Research (Hansen, 1986) and Alsted Research (1998) indicate that lone mothers are the only group in which poverty has increased dramatically during the past decade, and in Sweden the percentage of lone parents living below the poverty level (and receiving social assistance) doubled from 13% to 27% between 1991 and 1996 (Välfärdsprojektet, 1996).

Unemployment and gender discrimination

Unemployment across Europe has also disproportionately affected lone mothers, who experience the combined effects of gender discrimination in the workplace and the responsibilities of being both providers and nurturers for their children. Lone mothers in Denmark are the group with the highest unemployment rate (see Table 1). Their high unemployment rate also appears to be related primarily to levels of education (see Table 2). Additional factors pushing lone mothers into unemployment are a growing number of jobs with non-standard working hours and the lack of day care settings with flexible hours of operation within a reasonable proximity to their homes.

There is also a global disparity between the wages of men and women employees, and Denmark is no exception. In the 1990s the wage gap was 20% despite years of political declarations and legislation regarding equal pay (Smith and Naur, 1998). This wage gap directly influences the ability of lone mothers to earn a living wage through employment. Lone mothers living on meagre incomes benefit little, if at all, from low-wage employment, sometimes actually losing money when they move off social assistance and enter the labour market and find themselves with additional transportation and child care expenses to meet. Low wages in the gender-segregated labour market place many solo mothers, especially those without an education, in a well-known poverty trap as they do not earn adequate wages to allow for any surplus income once their daily living expenses are met. In addition, the stress of being a low-income solo parent coping with the constant pressures of maintaining a household with a deficit of temporal and financial resources, threatens the psychological health of the entire family unit. Juggling work and caring responsibilities, particularly when children become sick, frequently exacerbates the tenuous positions that lone mothers hold in the workplace (Folkhälsoinstituttet, 1994) as they face lost wages for absenteeism, or may be forced to stop working altogether to stay at home with a sick child.

In our study, contrary to prevailing stereotypes about the deficient work ethic of lone mothers and their habituated dependency, we did not find that unemployed lone mothers lacked the inclination or motivation to work; rather, low-wage employment simply did not 'pay', and for the women we interviewed, it often seemed less desirable and less practical an option, because mothers received a slightly higher monthly payment by staying on welfare and did not accrue additional work costs. In fact, for one of the mothers who was a part-time worker, the inflexible policy of limiting her supplement from unemployment benefits to two years had the net result of ousting her from the labour market and necessitating a return to welfare in order to survive.

Table 1: Position of Danish women in the labour market, distributed according to age, family status, and whether or not they have children, 1994 (%)

	Employed	Unemployed	Outside the labour force
20-29 years of age			
All women	67.2	14.0	18.8
Single without children	66.4	11.2	22.4
Single with children	44.2	25.8	30.0
Married/cohabitee without children	75.8	11.6	12.6
Married/cohabitee with children	64.1	18.1	17.8
30-39 years of age			
All women	77.8	10.9	11.3
Single without children	69.4	11.4	19.2
Single with children	63.2	18.1	18.7
Married/cohabitee without children	79.9	9.9	10.2
Married/cohabitee with children	81.6	9.6	8.8

Note: The proportion of women in the age group 20-29 who are employed, unemployed or out of the labour force varies significantly depending on their family status. Among lone mothers in this age group only 44% are employed while nearly 26% are unemployed and 30% are out of the labour force. The affiliation to the labour market is thus markedly weaker for single mothers than for both single women without children, and for mothers living in couples with or without children. Being out of the labour force refers to a broad array of possible activities, and a significant proportion of the women in the 20-29 age group who are registered as outside the labour force are currently pursuing education and will later be in gainful employment. Therefore, the information on employment, unemployment and position outside the labour force for women in the 30-39 age group gives a more realistic picture measuring the impact of family status and child caring responsibilities on women's labour market position. Comparing single mothers and mothers living in couples for this age group we find that the proportion of lone mothers who are unemployed and out of the labour force are, respectively, twice as high as /double the proportion among mothers living in couples.

Source: Danmarks Statistik (1994), calculated on the basis of combined registered information on family, education and the labour market status, compiled by Bodil Stensvig

Table 2: Position of Danish women in the labour market, distributed according to age, family status, and whether or not they have children (1994) (%)

	Employed	Unemployed	Outside the labour force
20-29 years of age			
Single without children			
no vocational education	56.4	12.2	31.5
vocational education	79.2	11.0	9.7
higher education	69.3	7.4	23.4
Single with children			
no vocational education	34.1	28.6	37.3
vocational education	65.8	20.8	13.4
higher education	60.3	10.9	28.8
Married/cohabitee without children			
no vocational education	63.1	14.9	22.0
vocational education	84.9	10.3	4.8
higher education	78.9	6.9	14.2
Married/cohabitee with children			
no vocational education	48.3	23.1	28.5
vocational education	77.3	14.8	7.9
higher education	79.5	7.3	13.2
30-39 years of age			
Single without children			
no vocational education	50.1	14.8	35.1
vocational education	82.4	9.7	7.9
higher education	85.6	7.7	6.7
Single with children			
no vocational education	48.9	23.5	27.6
vocational education	77.2	13.4	9.4
higher education	85.4	7.3	7.4
Married/cohabitee without children			
no vocational education	65.9	14.3	19.8
vocational education	88.6	7.8	3.6
higher education	90.7	5.3	4.0
Married/cohabitee with children			
no vocational education	70.0	14.4	15.6
vocational education	87.9	7.5	4.6
higher education	93.0	3.6	3.4

Note: No vocational education includes persons who have only completed the basic educational requirements such as 9th or 10th grade.

The position of women in the labour market is, however, not solely determined by their family status and whether they have children or not. Many international research studies indicate that education is a decisive factor influencing women's attachment to the labour market. The employment percentage is considerably lower for women who do not have an education than for women who do. This difference applies whether women have or do not have children, or whether they live alone or with a partner. However, lack of education seems to hit younger lone mothers particularly hard. Lone mothers, 20-29 years, without an education, compose the group which, out of all the groups of women, have the lowest rate of employment, the highest rate of unemployment, and the greatest percentage of women outside the labour force.

Source: Danmarks Statistik (1994), calculated on the basis of combined registered information on family, education and the labour market status compiled by Bodil Stensvig

Constant economic insecurity and environmental stress

All the lone mothers we interviewied were in a constant 'economic survival' mode, struggling to sustain their families, often against innumerable obstacles: one with a full-time low-wage job; one with a part-time low-wage job; three receiving rehabilitation (*revalidering*) education assistance under §43 (see Chapter 1, Note 2); one receiving unemployment benefits; one receiving SU[1]; and the rest receiving general social assistance (see Appendix B for the annual amounts of these benefits and the currency equivalents). Their daily household budgets were so tight that it was almost impossible to save money after paying for food, rent, day care, clothing, utilities and insurance. The stories the women tell about their everyday struggles to survive and "the constant going cap in hand" to the social assistance centre illustrate Habermas' juxtaposition between the life world and the system world (1971). Social assistance centres and the systems of which they are a part function according to rigid rules and procedures that are often indifferent to the fragile and turbulent private lives of lone mothers and their children. The families in our study live with unpredictable events which often cause unpredictable expenses, and many times the consequence is the collapse of an already tenuous household economy. According to the logic of the social welfare system, almost all life events are controllable and therefore should be anticipated so that expenses are planned and predictable. The law places the burden of responsibility on a lone mother in need of assistance to somehow predict her future needs and problems: she should predict, for example, that she will need baby equipment when she becomes pregnant, she should clairvoyantly foretell when second-hand appliances will wear out and break down, anticipate when her children will become sick, and most importantly, plan ahead if and when she escapes from a violent partner that such an action will incur extra expenses! As a result of this 'predictability' thinking, lone mothers may be denied help at social centres, despite provisions for support that exist in both the 1976 and 1998 laws governing social assistance.

Clearly, many unplanned crises, often precipitated by unstable living situations, occur in the lives of low-income lone mothers. Many of the mothers in our study, and social workers in private social organizations who have helped them, describe how difficult it is today to secure economic support from the public social welfare system for even the most rudimentary furnishings necessary to establish oneself in a new flat. Subsidies are generally refused, and even when a grant is given, the amount is so minimal that it is impossible to pay relocation expenses and buy basic necessities such as furniture, a stove, and a refrigerator. Under such circumstances many of the lone mothers choose survival strategies: taking bank loans and/or buying on installment, which precipitate a vicious spiral. Debts of about Dkr 100.000 are not uncommon, and escaping this debt will, for most of the mothers, be a daunting task in the foreseeable future.

Consequently, severe psychological stress and often hopeless burdens of debt push economically overwhelmed mothers to the margins of society. In today's social policy discussions about 'the new family' and ensuring each family's economic responsibility, it is expected that private support networks can and will assist with any crisis situation within the family; however, for many of the lone mothers portrayed in this book, either there is no network or the network members are themselves stretched so thin that the possibility of receiving economic and social support is unlikely, and frequently it is the breakdown of such family networks that precipitated the initial trauma and/or instability in the first instance. In addition, children living in families with ongoing economic insecurity and high environmental stress, including violence, are themselves scarred by the psychological toll that poverty and marginalization take on all family members, precipitating, for some, behavioural and academic problems during crucial developmental years.

Acute housing problems

The acute housing problems experienced by the mothers in our study echo the many unpredictable events and break-ups in their lives, but they are also clearly the disastrous consequences of being poor in a housing market with few affordable decent quality flats. All of the mothers in our study have experienced housing problems, some of an extremely serious nature, resulting, for example, in a period of homelessness for one woman and her son. Others have been forced to live in substandard housing completely unsuitable for a family, with damaging consequences to their children's health, contributing to chronic bronchitis, asthma and ear infections.

Many of the housing crises were experienced by mothers fleeing with their children from domestic violence, leaving behind furniture, clothing, kitchen appliances, toys and the carefully built material frames of family life. In some cases, mothers and children have later recovered their belongings, and in other cases possessions have been destroyed by their violent partners. Some mothers and children have been so emotionally damaged by domestic violence that they do not want to live with their former possessions, and have had to stay for months in a crisis centre, waiting for a suitable flat to become available.

A stable, safe and decent home is clearly a fundamental requirement for family stability. All other aspects that pertain to the quality of life, including having the energy and resources to care for one's children, the ability to enter the educational system and the labour market, depend on gaining access to safe, healthy, affordable housing. For the children of lone mothers, a stable home also means stability in relation to day care, school and friends, and the possibility of establishing social networks.

In the chapters that follow, the stories told by Hanne, Gina, Linda, Mona, Jette and Ditte are presented; stories that tell of low-wage dead-end work, sick children, bad housing, indifferent social centres, blocked access to education, and the constant struggle to survive with their children. It is through their stories that we learn much about social policy and practice on-the-ground – about whom it hurts and whom it helps.

Note

[1] SU: *Statens Uddannelsesstøtte* (Danish State Education Grant and Loan Scheme). The educational support system has been in force since the 1950s. The support consists of a combination of grants and government-subsidized loans. For students over 20 years the amounts per month are: grants (subject to tax) 3.907 Dkr and loans 2.031 Dkr (see Appendix B). SU is neutral for family size, which means that a student with children receives the same amount as a student without children.

THREE

Struggling against the odds

Hanne, Mark, and Søren

> "Lone mothers ... we are just regarded as one great grey mass in the
> social system – they do not know anything about my special situation
> and all the problems that have hit me and my children – and they do
> not care at all."

Thirty-five-year-old Hanne works full time as a low-wage worker in
the cafeteria of a large hospital. The low wages she earns barely
make ends meet for herself and her two sons, Mark (13 years) and
Søren (5 years). Hanne has worked since she left school after
completing the eighth class, and with no formal education, has always
held unskilled jobs. When her older son was six, after years of
enduring her husband Benny's drug addiction and violence, Hanne
left him, taking six-year-old Mark with her. Life has been very difficult
financially and emotionally for Hanne, and since her younger son
Søren was born, he has suffered from serious health problems. Hanne
and her children have not received much understanding or support
from the social centre nor from Mark's school, as she has struggled
to manage a precarious family life. Hanne lacks a supportive network,
and since the death of her grandmother and mother, both of whom
were close to her, she has become increasingly isolated. Hanne
describes her early years with Mark's father:

> "I got more and more tired of looking at Mark's father, Benny, sitting
> at home without work, just smoking hash/grass, drinking beer and
> playing with the computer while I went to work everyday.... Then
> my mother died, and I almost broke down from sorrow.... I told
> Benny that I would leave him, and I left for a few days to think
> things over. Mark stayed with Benny. Two days later a neighbour
> called me and said that Benny had gone crazy. I had to go back

home. When I returned, Benny hit me several times and threw me
backwards down the stairs.... Mark saw the whole thing and tried to
get in-between and defend me. Benny threw Mark against the wall.
At last the police came and took care of me and Mark.... Benny also
destroyed our furniture by throwing it out of the windows...."

Following this violent incident, Hanne decided not to go back to
Benny, so she took Mark and moved in with her new friend, John,
who "listened to all my sorrow about my mother's death and comforted
me and did all those things that Benny did not do".

A precarious family existence

Hanne and Mark lived with John for several months, but Hanne
decided to terminate the relationship, and discovering that she was
unexpectedly pregnant with Søren, she moved with Mark into a crisis
centre run by the private housing organization, Boligfonden. While
staying in that supportive environment, Hanne was able to talk about
and work through her feelings about her mother's death and the
domestic violence she had experienced when Benny attacked her.
Boligfonden also provided Hanne and Mark with a flat where they
went to live just prior to Søren's birth. Soon after they moved in,
Hanne and Mark witnessed the murder of a supermarket employee
at the hands of a mentally ill customer while they were shopping.
After this traumatic event, Hanne rushed home with eight-year-old
Mark. Soon Hanne began having labour pains even though her
baby was not expected for another six weeks. She went to the hospital,
and Søren was born after a long and painful childbirth. Hanne
experienced extremely insensitive treatment from the police, who
barged in on her just after the birth and even before the umbilical
cord was cut, to question her about the murder she and Mark had
witnessed. There were more and more questions from the police in
the weeks following her son's birth, and Hanne became a central
witness in the court proceedings. She was offered psychological
assistance, but she stopped going to therapy when she felt like the
psychologist "was getting too close".

The months following Søren's birth were an extraordinarily stressful
time for Hanne and her children. Søren went through several hernia
operations during his first seven months and also had feeding problems.

Hanne had to spend hours and days in the hospital with him, and Mark was jealous of all the time she was spending with his new brother. Mark also missed his biological father, Benny, whom he had not seen in two years since the incident of domestic violence that had prompted Hanne to leave. Hence Hanne contacted Benny and attempted to reestablish a relationship between Mark and his father. At this point, however, Hanne found herself embroiled in a new and stressful situation. Søren's biological father, John, who sometimes helped her take care of Mark and Søren, was accused by one of Hanne's neighbours of having sexually abused her nine-year-old daughter. John was found guilty and sentenced, but Hanne, who was convinced of his innocence, found an expert attorney to appeal his case. John was acquitted on appeal, but Hanne was completely worn down by the whole situation. Soon it became impossible for her to stay in her apartment with the same neighbours living near her. Boligfonden once again helped her find another apartment, where she and her children now live.

An isolated family

While Hanne continues to receive some assistance from John, she has no other network of family or friends to help her with her daily life. Her only brother and his girlfriend live too far away for them to see each other often. Hanne has always preferred to work and says she has never dreamed of staying home all day with her sons. She likes meeting and talking to other adults every day and finds this one of the advantages of going to work. Hanne says that even though she would receive an additional 800 Dkr each month (see Appendix B for currency equivalencies) if she did not work and, instead, received full social assistance, she would rather go to work and earn her own money, and apart from her two maternity leaves she has remained in the low-wage unskilled labour force. Outside of her working hours, Hanne is very much alone with her two boys and struggles to be a good mother and a good provider under severe economic and stressful emotional conditions, while relying on her older son to take care of Søren while she is at work. Hanne describes a typical morning for herself and her sons:

> "I wake up at 4.30 am and prepare lunches for the three of us. Then
> I dress Søren while he is half asleep. I leave home at 6.00 am for

work. At 7.00 am I call Mark on the telephone and wake him up. Mark dresses himself, then he wakes up Søren and walks with him to the kindergarten five minutes away where Søren eats his breakfast. Then Mark goes back home and eats his own breakfast before leaving for school just before 8.00 am.... After work, I spend some time alone with Mark and then pick up Søren, do the shopping, cooking, etc."

Hanne's budget is extremely tight, and she often finds it impossible to balance her expenses against her earnings. At night when her boys are sleeping Hanne spends an hour or two making decorations out of dried flowers. She sells them for a little extra income at Christmas time. This summer, for the first time, Hanne and her children have been invited by a private organization to take a one-week summer holiday together. But another private organization that has given Hanne food for her Christmas dinner for several years could not do so recently because the number of applicants had risen, and preference was given to lone mothers living on social assistance; hence once again Hanne experiences the double disadvantages of being a low-wage earner. In order to keep her family afloat, Hanne juggles debts and plays for time as part of her own system of survival. She has given up on paying her old debts (former flat, shopping account, back taxes, and so on), but instead goes to civil court twice each year where she explains her financial situation. Each time she leaves with her financial condition unchanged except for the increasing interest she owes on her debts.

Added to her economic burdens is the news that Søren has recently lost his free slot in his day care centre. Hanne is angry and embittered by the actions of the social centre as the free day care slot is permitted for pedagogical reasons, based on a child's need, and Hanne does not understand why the social centre believes these reasons no longer apply in Søren's case. Hanne recently attended an introductory course in her new role as a union representative in her workplace, and there she was informed about her rights to additional social assistance. To her chagrin, Hanne discovered that she was entitled to some benefits which the social centre never told her about, such as subsidies for her son's asthma medicine and bedwetting problem; and now that she is informed about her rights she fully intends to claim them. Hanne feels that the social workers at the social centre have been continually indifferent to her plight and have shown no sensitivity to the needs of her children.

Hanne and Mark

Mark, Hanne's oldest son, started attending a day care centre when he was one year old. During his first few years, Mark was a delicate child who suffered from many ear infections and had surgery to insert a drain into his ear. Until he was six years old Mark lived with both his parents; but after the incident of domestic violence, his parents divorced and Mark did not see his father again for two years. During those two years, Mark was traumatized by witnessing the murder of a stranger, and had to cope with his mother's unavailability when she was preoccupied and often overwhelmed by the serious health problems of his new-born brother, Søren. Mark also experienced several destabilizing moves with Hanne, and during that time he developed eating problems. When Søren's biological father was accused of sexually abusing a neighbour's daughter, the police questioned Mark several times, leading Mark to isolate himself in their flat until they moved once again.

Mark is now 13 years old, and through their shared traumatic experiences, Mark and Hanne have developed a very close relationship, and are extremely dependent on each other. Mark shoulders many adult responsibilities, which Hanne describes:

> "At home he is very helpful. He washes the dishes after dinner, takes Søren to kindergarten in the morning and picks him up again after school if I get delayed. He cooks potatoes for our dinner without being asked to do it. I find him more grown up and mature than his friends who are the same age. I think I also have talked with him when I have been worried about Søren's illnesses, and I am not sure that other parents do that, but I only have Mark to talk with. But I never involve him in my money problems. He is really aware of practical house chores, for instance he cleans up the bathroom saying, 'You have so much to do, Mother'. And he knows that if the house is not cleaned up during the week days, then we will have to do it on the weekends, when we like to have a nice cosy time."

Hanne says that Mark is very dependent on her and often clings so much that she becomes irritated by it. She finds him withdrawn and reserved, and he does not allow Hanne to intrude on his private world: "He never talks to me about his problems. He keeps everything to himself. When I ask him, he says that he does not want to bother talking about it".

Mark is often absent from school and his teacher sees his absence as a problem. Sometimes he is home taking care of his sick little brother; often he has stomach pains or just does not want to go to school, especially when his mother has a day off work and is at home. Mark is not an academically successful student, and has developed learning difficulties in several subject areas. He says:

> "I have extra classes in Danish, German, and English. I don't like being taken out of the classroom because I want to stay with my class. I am often away from school in order to help my mother with my brother or something else."

The insecurity and turbulence of his early childhood and the many chores and responsibilities placed on his shoulders have an obvious influence on Mark's poor school performance. However, Mark has not received adequate support at school, and the school staff appear to know very little about Mark's life outside of the classroom. His teacher for the last seven years comments:

> "Mark is sometimes very dull, but otherwise a nice boy who never talks back to me. He does not make trouble. He is a quiet boy and he seems to be a little insecure and cautious, but he does not have any behaviour problems.... He is a very responsible and mature boy.... I did not notice that the trial against Søren's father was such a problem for Mark, and I am surprised to hear that it was so hard for him and that he was not getting better help.... I cannot see that Mark feels he is different from his friends because he lives alone with his mother...."

Mark, who is never disruptive in school, largely drifts by unnoticed as he struggles academically, and remains socially isolated and 'adultified' at home. He fantasizes about his father with whom he has resumed a relationship and very much wants to remain connected to him, although the father is often drunk when Mark visits. When Mark turns 14, he will celebrate his confirmation, and expresses the hope he will be able to invite his father and all his father's 52 relatives to the celebration, although he has never met most of them. Mark still dreams of his parents getting back together:

> "My greatest wish is that my mother and father lived together again. It is the worst thing that has happened in my life when my father and

mother separated. I still hope it will be possible to be a family together again. I feel I am different from my friends because I live alone with my mother…."

Hanne and Søren

Hanne's pregnancy and Søren's early infancy were fraught with multiple traumas – Hanne's shock of witnessing a murder, premature labour, a court trial, and Søren's chronic health problems, necessitating three hernia operations. During one of the operations Søren did not wake up from the anaesthesia, and Hanne had him baptized for fear he would die. After he recovered he developed an eating disorder and Hanne would sometimes make him sit at the dinner table for up to one-and-a-half hours in order to get him to eat some food. Hanne recalls those stressful times:

> "Søren has experienced so much while I had him in my belly. I do not know how much it has influenced him. But at the time of the court case against his father he was only 18 months old…. Still, today Søren is very much a mother's boy, and we are closely attached to each other. I am sure that deep down at a subconscious level, Søren knows that things have happened in his life which tie the two of us together today…. Søren cannot sleep alone in a dark room. He sleeps beside me, and to fall asleep he wants me to lie at his side so that he can hold some of my hair in his hands. He has never slept without me…. His dependency on me irritates me a little, for I also have to spend time with Mark."

When he turned one, Hanne enrolled Søren at a family day care home as she prepared to return to work, but this proved traumatic for Søren: "Even though I was away from my job for more than two months trying to make a flexible start for him in the day care home, he just cried from the time I left until I came back again". The day care provider could not handle this situation, and three months later Hanne switched Søren to a day care centre where he made a better adjustment. He has since developed asthma and is on constant medication which has damaged his teeth and physically marred his appearance:

> "Nobody told me that the medicine would totally destroy his teeth, and so I did not know that I should have brushed his gums carefully

when he was a baby. Søren went to a dentist who ground his teeth down and filled them with some black stuff which is not nice to look at. I am so sorry about it because he is often teased about his black teeth in the kindergarten."

Søren also suffers from psoriasis and regularly wets his bed, which Hanne feels is a reaction to his stressful young life, although his doctor thinks that the bedwetting may be caused by the operations he had when he was an infant. Søren is overattached to his mother, so much so that Hanne finds it is a growing problem: "He is constantly clinging to me. I cannot do anything without having him with me. I cannot go to the toilet or take a bath without him. I find him extremely demanding. He often has stomach pains in the morning and will not leave home".

Søren's pedagogue at his day care centre shares her observations:

"Søren gets very upset when things change around him, it makes him very anxious.... Søren is almost being taken care of too much. Søren and his mother have a very close relationship. His mother does not have any freedom. She has given up much of her own life in order to take care of her children. Søren is very upset when he arrives in the morning, and it is difficult for him to let his mother leave. Afterwards, he spends hours by himself, and it is hard for him to concentrate and engage in any activity. He sometimes asks about his mother the whole day long. But at the same time, I have to say that it is surprising that Søren does not have even more problems considering his background and all the severe troubles his family has had."

Søren has not made friends at day care, and he has difficulty playing and engaging in any activities with other children. He appears to feel insecure and lacks confidence. An observation we made of Søren at the centre playground is illustrative:

On the playground, one of the children, Jan, is sitting on the ball and will not give it to Søren and neither does he want to play with him. Søren speaks to Jan quietly several times but without success. For a long time Søren circles around him, but nothing happens. Søren does not complain or get angry. Then Søren circles around the other boys playing football, but he does not join their play. He comes over and tells me that his friend does not want to play. I encourage him to ask his friend again, but Søren does not do this. Then he tells a pedagogue [that Jan does not want to play with him] who tells him to do the same. Søren does not; he appears afraid of the conflict and instead goes to a corner of the playground where he starts swinging alone.

Hannah, Mark and Søren face their future

Hanne is fighting for her family's survival – she has succeeded in keeping a job despite her lack of education, the severe health problems of her children, and the many traumas in her private life. She is in every respect responsible for her sons, for their growing up in general, their health and education, and their relationships with their fathers. But Hanne seems to be completely alone as she endures a string of traumatic events and problems in her life with no social network to turn to. She feels that she has been callously treated at the social centre and that her situation has neither been understood nor assisted by her social workers in the public system. She is under constant financial stress and feels hounded. To survive she seeks help from private organizations. She is concerned about both her sons, for Mark's learning difficulties and stomach pains, and Søren's emotional and health problems, appear directly related to the severe economic and emotional stress endured during critical phases of their development. The social system and the school system have either not known about or not realized the significance of these difficult experiences, and therefore they have offered little assistance or support to Hanne and her children. Thus far Hanne has proven to be a resilient survivor, but chronic and long-term stress may erode the energies and resources of even the strongest of lone mothers.

Gina, Jon and Gabriella

"I asked for help since 1992, but no one heard me. It is my experience that you have to be very badly off before they help. I asked and asked for help and I didn't get it until I was totally down...."

Gina is the 28-year-old mother of nine-year-old Jon, and two-and-a-half-year-old Gabriella. Gina experienced a very difficult and abusive childhood and young adulthood. She has been in the social system for over 10 years and has been the victim of domestic violence perpetrated by the father of one of her children. During her years as a lone mother, she has experienced severe housing problems, and her children have been sick constantly with bronchial ailments. Her son has been diagnosed as hyperactive and is a source of continuing anxiety as Gina has struggled to hold their lives together.

Growing up in an abusive family

Gina's father is Italian and her mother is Danish. Her parents divorced when she was a young child, and soon afterwards her father returned to Italy. Gina describes being taunted at school because of her mixed ethnic background and appearance, "I was spat upon, beaten, and taunted, 'You black thing, you smell, you shit, you get out of the country...'". Gina and her younger sister continued to live in Denmark with their mother with whom Gina had a bad relationship and who she now describes as "not a good mother ... definitely not". Gina relates how, because she "was the big one at home", she also had to take care of and cook for her younger sister, taking on 'mother' responsibilities. When Gina was 14 years old her mother became involved with a man who was often drunk, and he beat and sexually molested Gina. She ran away from home and went to a youth centre and stayed there for two years. This was a very traumatic period of Gina's adolescence:

> "My mother has done things that I am not proud of ... they were always on drugs and drinking and everything, and it was horrible. It was very bad because I had to arrange money for feeding me and my sister, and he was always looking at us and telling us, 'Now I've done this and that to your mother sexually – what do you think about that', and I mean I hadn't even had my first sexual experience, and we were always saying, 'This is disgusting, is this what sex is about'...."

> "I don't remember very much of that time ... it was such a bad time. I think that is also why I go to the psychologist, just to remember, because I need to open up ... because if I'm doing things now because of what happened then.... I try to be as whole as possible so I don't leave my children with all this trash in their life...."

As Gina relates her traumatic adolescence, she expresses guilt for leaving her sister after she ran away, stating that after she left, her mother's boyfriend "smacked her [sister] every day.... When I was there with my sister, he didn't touch her, he was after me". When the man began molesting Gina and she fought him back, she told her mother, but her mother failed to respond and protect her daughter:

> "And I tried to tell my mother and she would smack me and say, 'Don't tell me this kind of nonsense'. But later on I found out that she had the same kind of problems at home [when she was a child] and her mother reacted the same way ... and I understand her now, but that doesn't mean I accept her way of doing things...."

At present Gina is estranged from her mother whom she describes as completely indifferent to her children: "[She] never ever once asked to have the children for a couple of hours, or says, 'Let me pick them up or let me buy them something nice'". Gina also relates that her mother recently celebrated a 50th birthday party and she was told not to bring the children:

> "... because she said it wasn't allowed to have children at the party. And when I came the place was full of [other] children ... so she's never going to do that to me again ... and then of course I was so happy that we didn't make a speech ... we were supposed to make a speech for her, and the silence was the speech. We couldn't find anything positive to say...."

Struggling to survive as a lone mother

Gina's young adult life has been chaotic. She has had to confront a series of stressful events, resulting from her relationships with the fathers of her two children – severe housing problems, escalating debts, and domestic violence. She has no supportive social network, and her sister with whom she had a close relationship recently left the country to live abroad.

When Gina was 18 she met Jon's father, and a year later she gave birth to Jon. Jon's father drank and smoked hashish and did not work, while Gina, taking care of her baby son, had to work at two jobs:

"I worked in an after school centre from 11.30-4.30, and at 5 I had another work [job] where I was packing comic books and magazines and everything. And I got off the job at 12 o'clock midnight, and it took me one-and-a-half hours to get home, and I had to get up in the morning, make sure Jon got to kindergarten, preparing food for him and paying the bills and shopping and then going to work. So I was pretty exhausted and he was just sitting home...."

Gina's boyfriend was also consistently late and irresponsible about picking up their son from day care while she was at work, and after she was called one evening at work to pick up Jon because his father had failed to show up, she decided to leave him:

"And when I picked up Jon I went home and he was lying on the couch, sleeping, and smelling of the booze so badly ... so I said to him, 'No, now I'm leaving you if you don't pull yourself together, and you don't help paying the rent, and you don't help pay the bills, then I will move'. And he thought I was kidding. But I had to move because I could not stand it any longer."

After she left with Jon, Gina was saddled with many debts from her boyfriend, who, she says, ruined her economically. Gina's nightmare housing odyssey began as she searched for a flat encumbered by the many debts incurred during the previous relationship with her boyfriend. She lived in several unsatisfactory places, moved frequently and became involved with another boyfriend who was abusive. While living with her abusive boyfriend in a flat with no kitchen (she had to use a fireplace for cooking), no hot water, and only one heated area (which meant that she had to buy electric heaters which caused high heating bills), one of the tenants began selling drugs: "And I was saying, my God this is nothing I want to live in. So I moved very quickly.... And I went up to the crisis centre and I was crying and saying what am I going to do. I'm going to stand in the street in four hours. Help!" After a nine-month stay at the crisis centre with her son, Gina attempted, but failed, to end the relationship with her abusive boyfriend:

"I was not able to get out of this relationship, because I was more afraid of letting him go than to stay with him. Because he would be very violent; if I said, 'Go away', he would be there all the time ... so it wasn't very nice, but I couldn't get rid of him even there, because

they were saying to me, 'You have to get rid of him'. And when they
said that in that way, I protested...."

After she was offered a flat by the social housing agency, Gina had to
leave the crisis centre although she was very reluctant to take the flat
as there was no heating, no bath, and no hot water, and she had to
use the sink to bathe her son, who was now almost five years old.

> "I had no choice and I wasn't on the street and that was definitely a
> good thing. But it felt very strange to be let go of ... the only thing I
> had to do at the crisis centre was sleep, take care of the food and my
> child and myself, and that made space for me to focus on my needs...."

Gina continued to live a precarious existence, struggling to make
ends meet and falling further and further into debt. In addition her
son, diagnosed as hyperactive, required special foods, which increased
her costs. She became pregnant by her abusive boyfriend, and gave
birth to her daughter, Gabriella. During this time she appealed on
several different occasions to the social centre for help, but found
them unresponsive and insensitive to her desperate economic needs.
She was unable to work because both children suffered from chronic
bronchitis and asthma due to the damp cold flat, and when Gina
found another flat, the social centre told her they wouldn't pay for it
as it was too expensive, despite the fact that her doctor wrote a letter
saying that it was necessary for her to move on account of the children's
health problems. Because of her bad debts Gina could not manage
to rent anything on her own, describing herself during that time as
"desperate" and "really freaking out", feeling that "I can never get
out of this". Eventually, after several years of these severe housing
problems, Gina turned to Boligfonden for help, and they assisted
her in finding her current flat which is spacious and well heated.

During the years that Gina was living in substandard housing, and
becoming increasingly desperate about Jon's hyperactivity and both
children's constant bouts of sickness, she was also a victim of
psychological and physical abuse by Gabriella's father.

Coping with domestic violence

Gina describes the psychological abuse that began after Gabriella's
birth:

"He had done it in the sense that he played with my mind. He was doing tricks on my mind ... and I wouldn't notice until after, and he would say, 'Oh you must be a psycho-bitch since you always turn around what you want and you don't want'. And I was thinking, maybe I am, maybe there is something wrong with my mind. And I started to believe it...."

Several months later, Gina became ill with a severe nerve infection in her face which was very painful:

"I couldn't touch my skin without screaming ... and he said to me I was just hysterical, and I was saying, 'Oh my god this is insane ... he said because I am mad that I get this'. But the first punch he gave me was exactly in all this [in my face], and then he broke my ear inside by smacking me and trying to strangle me ... and while he was kicking me around I picked up the 'phone and dialled the police, and he didn't know what number I was 'phoning ... but they heard what he was saying and they heard me screaming ... so they tracked it and 10 minutes later there was police everywhere ... and they told him, 'You get out of this house now. If you don't get out we will take the children and put them in a home...'."

While the police arrive promptly and witness the end of the assault, they do not arrest the perpetrator, but rather threaten to remove the children which clearly would further victimize Gina, rather than punish her boyfriend. Significant too is the fact that Gina is afraid to press charges against him, as he threatens to retaliate because she cut his arm when he was attacking her. So he suffers no repercussions. However, Gina's friends take measures and beat him up, and she ends the relationship, but he continues to see his daughter weekly. While Gina describes the assault very vividly as a terrifying time, she seems to see no possible danger in terms of his relationship with her young daughter, despite the fact that his uncontrollable physical violence and past psychological abuse indicate a dangerous individual. Gina appears to have accepted his "apologizing" and describes him as "completely in love" with Gabriella, saying "he lets her do anything".

At the time of interviewing Gina, Gabriella is two-and-a-half years old and has started attending a day care centre. However, as Gina is preoccupied with Jon's hyperactivity and severe emotional problems, the focus of the following section is on Jon's complicated and unstable home life, and his rejection by his father.

Jon's world

Gina dates the beginning of Jon's problems to a severe adverse reaction to a vaccination at about 15 months. Gina describes how, prior to the vaccination:

> "... he walked fine, talked a little but then he got that injection and his language disappeared and his motor function went wrong. I complained to the doctor but he said the vaccination couldn't be the cause ... but Jon's development changed, his whole way of behaving changed, his language did not come back until he was three-and-a-half years old ... he started day care and they kept saying Jon had problems ... he had difficulties in a group – they didn't do anything about it ... even more fights and conflicts appeared ... no one could touch him or say something to him or change his play ... otherwise he would go bananas ... and at that time no one gave me any help ... and I thought maybe he was sad, that he missed his father ... that it was some way of expressing his protest as Jon had not seen his dad for a long time...."

Jon's early childhood was difficult as they lived in very unstable housing arrangements, his father was indifferent and rejecting, and Gina describes Jon as "missing his father" and how his father "has not wanted to see him" and has let him down on numerous occasions when he has not shown up for a visit. Jon's day care experience was not positive, and he did not receive the supportive interventions he needed as his condition appeared to worsen. He received several incomplete and inconclusive psychological evaluations while attending day care, and it was suggested that he had brain damage. When Jon began preschool class, Gina was dissatisfied and switched him to another preschool, but that also proved to be problematic. A boy attacked Jon at preschool and when Gina complained, she was told that she was the problem. She impulsively moved him again, this time to a private school, based on the recommendation of a young male friend who had attended that school whose motto was "Try the strong arm of love". However, this school proved to be even worse for Jon:

> "He came home and told me that the teacher hits the kids and kicks them ... then I asked the teacher and he admitted it and said it was because the kids didn't obey ... then I ask for a meeting with the

> headmaster, four teachers and me ... but they don't talk about the teacher's behaviour at all, only about Jon and how bad he is doing ... then Jon stayed home for 11 days ... they wanted a psychologist to look at him, we trained at home ... then I called after 11 days but they had long waiting lists.... I asked for how long he must stay home ... then a week before summer holiday they told me they didn't want to see him anymore...."

After a series of further problems with a negligent school psychologist who did not see Jon for over two years, Gina complained to the district supervisor who advised her to lodge a complaint about the school. Finally Jon was diagnosed as having ADHD (attention deficit hyperactivity disorder). However, this only occurred after another critical episode when Jon was sent home a week before the class was due to go on a camping trip and he was told not to return. Gina was informed by the headmaster that Jon could not join the class on the camping trip, but should meet at the headmaster's office every day. Gina complained, saying that they could have arranged to have an extra pedagogue on the trip to deal with Jon, but the staff did not want Jon on the trip. Gina should also have been informed within a week about an alternative school placement for Jon, but due to the lack of information and faulty communication from the school, she kept him at home for almost two months. Only then did she find out that Jon was entitled to attend a school for special education students and he transferred. Jon likes his new school, and Gina is very pleased with the teachers and the support that he receives both at the school and at the afterschool programme. However, Jon is very vulnerable, and continues to exhibit many stress behaviours related to his unstable home life and his father's rejection of him. He wanted to go and live with his father, but his father refused, and Jon continues to idealize him and wants a better relationship but is constantly rejected by him. Gina relates what happened:

> "It's desperate ... he so much wants his love ... Jon wrote a letter sometime ago and asked why he didn't like him ... [saying] 'Do you think I'm stupid dad? Why don't you want to see me?... I like you so much.... Why don't you like me when I like you?'"

Jon also has a very conflictual relationship with Gina, who describes his out-of-control anger and his inability to handle frustrating situations:

"It can be anything ... he pushes everyone aside ... he made a scene in a shop the other day ... because I wouldn't buy him food right away ... and he had just got a pair of shoes ... he screamed ... he wanted that feta cheese ... he went crazy ... he wanted that feta cheese right now ... he cried aloud and he made me cry in the store ... screamed and called me a fat woman and whore ... I told him to go outside and wait ... then today I discovered I had a peach in my bag, and I gave it to him but that was not what he wanted so he screamed and went crazy ... then out of the store ... on my way out, one of the shop ladies gave me a clap on my shoulder and I started crying...."

While Gina has made Jon 'her priority' and has struggled to cope with his needs and behaviour problems, she readily acknowledges that, "I haven't been able to manage very well, no matter how much I've tried ... [sometimes] I can't manage at all and Jon has gone down with me ... he has been influenced by it all". In the Christmas of 1997, the stress on Gina was enormous, she was facing severe economic difficulties and described her situation:

"They told me I was not able to create a structured day for Jon – but how could I? I was so tired and I never had any money ... every day was a fight to get money, a fight to get up in the mornings ... I was so tired and exhausted I almost couldn't do anything ... that's why I couldn't set the limits he needs because he is an ADHD child and I've said it many times, what the hell should I do ... and then suddenly they wanted someone to come and visit me once a week and tell me what to do ... then I got really nervous.... It started at Christmas and I broke ... I had 320 Dkr to celebrate Christmas ... then in January they found out I had got too little money in December. At that time I even considered becoming a criminal or prostituting myself ... I said that to the social centre and then I got some notes so I could buy food at the supermarket. It was the most humiliating thing I have ever experienced ... the shop lady shouted through the whole store that I couldn't buy alcohol or cigarettes with the notes. I knew that.... The first and second time I almost crawled out of the shop, but the third time I told her off."

After the humiliation and stigmatization that Gina suffers in public, she once again seeks help from the social centre, and at this point, she finds a supportive response from a new social worker:

"She said, 'Listen, Jon suffers from you being so stressful'.... I didn't
have the patience and of course Jon is marked by it ... and they say
Jon is doing bad and then she [the social worker] started talking to
me about letting Jon stay at foster parents ... it's all voluntary for me
... at first I got really scared but then I listened to her and I go home
and talk to Jon about it.... I want him to be open and honest with
me, I'm his mother and I don't want anything to hinder him telling
me what he really thinks...."

Jon responds that he would like to stay at his grandmother's place or
at his father's, but neither of these are possible options, so he requests
his 'weekend family'[1], and the couple volunteer to serve as foster
parents. Early in 1998 Jon moves to the foster parents and at the
current time of writing has been living there for three months, having
just celebrated his 11th birthday in April 1998. The separation is
very difficult for Gina who finds the foster parents too strict and
"sharp" and not much "fun", but Jon comes home every third
weekend, and from the accounts of his teachers and pedagogues and
foster parents he seems to be progressing well.

Jon now has an integrated support system comprised of his teacher,
a social worker, counsellor, special pedagogue, Jon's foster parents,
and Gina, and there are regularly scheduled meetings to discuss Jon's
progress. Jon's teacher at the special education school he attends
reports that Jon has changed: "He is happier and feels good about
himself, he is very open, hard-working and very happy about his
own progress". The teacher comments that Jon is still very vulnerable,
describing him as, "a nice boy, funny, friendly, but hard to handle",
adding insightfully, "we don't use the diagnosis ADHD a lot, maybe
it's good for the parents, we know the theories but we look at the
children as normal people". The special needs pedagogue at the
afterschool programme confirms the teacher's assessment of Jon and
adds that Jon has experienced many disruptions in his young life,
and that he functions best with sensible limits and is doing well with
his foster parents. They are both working professionals with no
children of their own, and they have already served as Jon's 'relief'
family for almost two years. In an interview, they remark that Gina
has been very isolated, particularly since her sister left Denmark. They
are involved with Jon's school life and say they have never experienced
problems with him, as their home situation is far more structured:

"Here we have limits and things are stable and calm ... that was part of the problem when he was at home.... Since he moved in here things are better in school ... he has started reading ... he cries out for limits ... his breakfast, lunch and dinner ... here he is not allowed to sit in front of the TV as he did at home."

Jon is observed at his foster parents' home and is smiling, relaxed and friendly. He is excited about going fishing with his foster parents on the weekend, and although he has only spent three months there, he tells that he has been staying there for about a year. He likes their dog and the children in the neighbourhood, and appears to have adjusted well to his foster parents' home, where he has his own room with a new desk, bed, and computer games. When asked about school, he happily states, "now I read very well", and talks about his teacher who he likes very much, and that he is at "a good school". At his afterschool centre, he proudly states that he is "the leader" where he has climbed a very high 20 metre wall. During the conversation he is both attentive and calm.

The overall impression of Jon is that he is now in a stable environment, and is responding well to his changed situation. He receives intensive interventions by a coordinated support team of teachers, counsellors and social workers. His social and academic competence is progressing, but he still behaves very aggressively when upset. His ongoing rejection by his biological father continues to be a source of internal conflict as well as his relationship to his mother's new boyfriend and the boyfriend's five-year-old son. However, it is also clear that Jon has suffered enormously from the lack of educational and social support services that he was entitled to, but did not receive, for many years of his young life. These crucial services were not in place at many pivotal moments in this vulnerable young boy's life, and it is only in the past year that Jon has received the help that he needs.

Gina and her children in the future

Gina's new flat, obtained with the help of Boligfonden Housing Foundation, is pleasant and spacious, and for the first time in her adult life, Gina has found a stable and adequate living environment for herself and her children. Jon shows promising signs of progress, and Gina is now in a new relationship with a boyfriend whom she describes as supportive, while she still struggles to cope with her guilt and sense of loss about Jon. She has a job at a petrol station and is earning a little more money than she received on welfare, she is pleased to be working, saying, "I've also had more energy since I started working ... it's been good for me to have the job now Jon is gone.... I used to go to bed crying and I got up in the mornings crying...."

Gina continues to feel bitter about the fact that it took so long to get the help she needed, saying: "I asked for help since 1992, but no one heard me. It is my experience that you have to be very badly off before they help". Now that Gina is also receiving psychological help from a social counsellor at her social centre, she hopes to create a more stable and structured environment for her son to return to in the future – this may, however, take several years. Her economic situation continues to be marginal and is not likely to change significantly unless she receives some additional educational training. While Gina describes her new boyfriend as supportive, she remains very isolated, with a weak social network, particularly since her sister left the country two years ago. The fact that both her children were sick constantly during their early years with asthmatic bronchitis aggravated by their poor housing conditions, and that Gina had to cope with Jon's hyperactivity and behavioural problems alone for many years, prevented her from establishing herself in the labour market or from pursuing an education. In addition, Gina's history of psychological and physical traumas through her own adolescence and adulthood clearly helped to shape a vulnerable individual who was failed in multiple ways by a social system, which failed to act as she and her son fell through the many cracks in the social safety net. As an economically and psychologically vulnerable lone mother, she continues to struggle to survive.

Linda and Nicolaj

"For a long time I had anxiety attacks which paralysed me completely. I had to ask somebody to call me in the morning to be sure that I woke up again because of my death anxiety. I am enormously afraid of having a heart attack. It has been going on for several years with this panic. Now I am better.... I can get very nervous and become overwhelmed by bad and stupid thoughts, but today I can get out of these situations by myself. I have not taken any medication for the last year, but I have the pills as security for myself."

Thirty-year-old Linda lives alone with her son, Nicolaj, who is four. When Nicolaj was born, and during the first year of his life, Linda developed acute anxiety, which she dates back to her childhood: "… it has been inside me long before. I have carried it in me for years, because of my relationship with my parents".

Surviving childhood

Although both of her parents are no longer alive, Linda sees her childhood and youth as greatly influenced by her parents' conflicted and unhappy marriage and divorce. Linda and her sister had an extremely strict upbringing, which Linda describes as psychologically abusive, with some occasional physical abuse in the form of spanking. Linda commented,

> "I didn't dare ask any questions … we never talked with each other in my family.… I have never had any relationship with my mother. I was a mistake for her. I should never have been born … my mother considered me a problem child."

Both parents had severe drinking problems and Linda believes that her mother committed suicide. Most of Linda's thoughts about growing up are bitter memories of alcoholism and family conflicts. Even today, Linda reported, she is sensitive to people just drinking a beer, and she is very particular that her home is always clean and neat. Linda feels isolated and alone and regrets the fact that she has never had adult people in her life with whom she could talk, and who could give her advice about daily living.

Linda has sought help from the public health system for her anxiety and mental health problems, but she has not been satisfied:

> "The only help you can get is a psychiatrist. She gave me some pills … and after having been in group therapy, I think it was five times, she then declared that I was fine. How could I be fine when I needed all these pills? From my own doctor I got some anti-anxiety medicine, but it is dependency-developing medicine."

Linda, in desperation, has also sought alternative treatments for her anxiety. When she called an astrology-based crisis hot-line, she was referred to a private therapist who uses the rebirth approach to dealing with anxiety. Linda has been to see this therapist about ten times, and she feels that the techniques have been very helpful. Linda said that she has always had difficulty expressing her feelings, that she does not cry easily, and that the intensive breathing exercises involved with rebirth therapy relieved much of her tension. Even though the therapy helped Linda, she still could not afford to pay the private therapist, and the social centre refused to help her. Linda's sister loaned her the 7,000 Dkr she needed to pay for the therapy.

Struggling to juggle work with being a lone mother

Like many lone mothers, Linda is responsible for both nurturing and providing for her child. While she was trained as a shop assistant, she has not worked in this area for many years. After Nicolaj's birth, Linda had a clerical job at a local nursing home. She liked the job, and appreciated the fact that her boss allowed her to bring Nicolaj with her to work when he was sick. But when she experienced an emotional crisis and suffered a nervous breakdown, she was fired and felt embittered that she received so little understanding and support from her employer.

Linda is determined that Nicolaj's childhood be different from her own. Cognizant of her emotional fragility, Linda recognizes how important it is not to get stressed and overwhelmed so that she can control her anxiety and be an attentive mother to Nicolaj. Since Nikolaj was born, she has worked part time, which has enabled her to spend more time with Nikolaj while receiving an unemployment benefit supplement to her wages to make up for the missing hours of work. But Linda finds herself caught in a typical low-wage lone-mother dilemma: the part-time supplement has come to an end, and her part-time salary excludes her from receiving social assistance which causes her a great deal of economic hardship. Linda, commenting on her experiences with the social centre states: "I do not get any help at all from them – not any help worth a shit". While Linda and Nicolaj now live in a modern flat with pleasant outdoor surroundings, Linda pointedly remarks that it was the social worker from a *private* housing agency that helped her obtain the flat:

"When I came to the office [at Boligfonden] to apply for the flat and we were sitting and talking, I suddenly felt that the social worker there was someone with whom I felt confident and to whom I dared to talk. He was outside the social system, and he understood what I was talking about. I told him about my anxiety ... that I was breaking down ... that I could not manage any longer. He simply sat down and went on listening to me ... I cannot cry ... but he is a person with whom I dare cry."

Linda finds herself living in a state of constant economic stress, and she struggles to figure out how increases and decreases in her income, resulting from her part-time work situation, affect her housing benefit and payments at Nicolaj's day care centre. She receives child support from Nicolaj's father, but he never offers to pay any extra money, and she is still struggling to pay back a former debt of 60,000 Dkr which she incurred when the relationship with Nikolaj's father ended.

Isolated and alone

Linda is very fond of her only sister who has helped her financially by loaning her the money she needed to pay for private, alternative treatment for her anxiety. Linda's sister is herself a lone mother, but because of the great geographical distance between them, there are often long periods of time when they do not see each other. With the exception of her sister, Linda has neither family nor friends she can turn to for help in a crisis, and she spends most of her free time with Nikolaj at home, remarking, "I think maybe I hold Nicolaj a little bit too close to me ... you miss another grown-up to see a movie with and have a cosy time with ... you only sit alone".

Claus, Nicolaj's father, is "like another child in the house" to Linda, and he sometimes fails to show up when he has promised Nicolaj that he will come over. Claus is six years younger than Linda, and in Linda's opinion he is very dependent on his own parents in almost every way. Claus just recently moved into his own flat, but he has not yet arranged a bed there for Nicolaj so all visits between Nicolaj and Claus take place in Linda's flat. Linda is thinking about establishing contact with a weekend family so that Nicolaj can sometimes stay with them, but she acknowledges it will be very difficult for her to separate from Nikolaj and leave him in their care. But she recognizes that she too needs an opportunity to do something for herself: "I also have to get care.... I may get a chance to find a man ... I have not gone out with anyone during the last 12 months".

Nicolaj's early years

Nicolaj's birth was a chaotic event for Linda. She had a long and difficult labour and Nicolaj was born with the help of a cupping-glass. His heart beat was faint and he was blue and limp, but after spending some time in an incubator, he soon recovered. From the first days of Nikolaj's fragile life, Linda was acutely anxious about taking care of him alone:

> "At three weeks old, he simply stopped breathing. If I had not discovered it, he would have died.... He was in my arms in the ambulance, but he was breathing very irregularly. They put an alarm on him, to monitor his breathing."

After this traumatic event, Nicolaj wore a baby monitor until he was eight months old. These first eight months of Nicolaj's life were exhausting for Linda, and she describes never getting a full night's sleep. Nikolaj's father, Claus, was indifferent: "Claus never registered or heard anything at all.... He did not help at all with Nicolaj ... he just went to his job". Without help from Nicolaj's father or any of her own family members, Linda's anxiety increased and her relationship with Claus "became very bad". As Linda looks back on those early months, and her overwhelming sense of aloneness, she tells:

> "Daily life with Nicolaj has been hard. I could hardly wait to take him to the infant centre so that I could have some time alone, and at the same time I didn't dare to be by myself.... When you have anxiety, you lose your life energy along with optimism and feeling full of life. For instance, cooking cannot engage you. Many times when I was cooking I felt very sick. I became nauseous and dizzy, and I became anxious and everything. But I continued, because Nicolaj has to have his food. In a way, the only thing that has kept me up is Nicolaj."

When Nicolaj was eight months old, the health visitor[2] diagnosed a squint in one of his eyes. Nicolaj has had to wear a patch over his normal eye at different times in his early years in order to train the other eye. He has also had recurring ear infections which necessitated a drain being surgically placed in his ear, and he was diagnosed as hearing impaired, and needs to have his ears checked every three months. Linda contacted a psychologist who reassured her about Nicolaj's health, and gave her good advice about handling Nikolaj's temper tantrums: "She was a mature woman.... I have not had a mother to talk to and get advice from.... I have missed having a mother".

Linda is aware of Nikolaj's extreme dependence on her and tries to encourage him to become more independent as she recently bought him a new bed and fixed up a room just for him. However, he still refuses to sleep alone. After spending more than two years at his infant centre, Nicolaj has just started at a new day care centre, and appears to be adjusting well and coping with the separation when Linda drops him off, describing him as, "much calmer after we have separated. He is not hysterical now".

Nicolaj at his day care centre

The day care pedagogue and Linda both report that Nicolaj is articulate and communicates well with adults and children. His language development is good, and he uses a large vocabulary with complex sentence construction, but lisps when he uses certain consonants. Linda is concerned he may need speech therapy, but right now they are heavily burdened with medical appointments with both eye and ear doctors. Nikolaj is open and warm in his interactions with the adults at his day care centre and the pedagogue's perception of Nicolaj is that he is a sensitive and insecure child who, for example, cannot tolerate dirt and "washes his hands much more than other children do". Linda corroborates Nikolaj's aversion to dirt and states: "Earlier, Nicolaj was very much afraid of getting dirty, but now it is better. Before, he wanted to change his t-shirt as soon as there was just a little bit of dirt. I gave him some finger paints, but he would not touch them....."

Nicolaj enjoys playing with the other children in day care, but he does not initiate play and has a little trouble staying in the game. He prefers to follow the lead of the other children and does not assert himself if he is annoyed or even hit by another child. Some examples from observing him at his day care centre are illustrative:

Nicolaj is playing with his friend but suddenly leaves, as he also did earlier, because he notices a woman he knows and wants to give her a hug. After a few minutes, Nicolaj returns to the game which has now changed. His friend has a new idea: now the beer boxes are loud speakers. Nicolaj resumes playing without commenting on this change. Another friend starts throwing the boxes and destroys the game. Nicolaj does not seem to notice, and he steps aside without complaining, even though the game is destroyed.... One of the other children hits Nicolaj in the head, but Nicolaj does not react.

Nicolaj has difficulty expressing his feelings and Linda and the pedagogue both report that Nicolaj almost never cries. The pedagogue remarks:

"It is hard for Nicolaj to keep his concentration when playing. He is usually very attentive to the other children and does not like it when they are sad. Then he wants them to be comforted. This attention to others, in reality, disturbs his playing and makes it hard for him to concentrate."

Linda is concerned about Nicolaj's lack of ability to assert himself, both in playing with his friends and in relation to her:

"Nicolaj is constantly being sat upon and oppressed by them [the other children], and he does not assert himself. He has also had too much respect for me, often much too much, and he does not stand up for himself. He is following my wishes too much.... When I correct him, he at once says, 'Are you angry with me, mother?' I am sad about this reaction and find it a bit strange."

Despite the concerns about Nicolaj, both Linda and his pedagogue have much to say about Nicolaj's strengths. His mother describes him as, "an extremely nice boy, very beautiful. His strong side is his charm, his ability to be careful, and his empathic feelings". Nicolaj's pedagogue comments about his ability to care for others, his openness, and his large vocabulary: "Nicolaj is a good friend, he shares with others, and I believe that he will develop himself into a child with whom the other children like to play".

The future for Linda and Nicolaj

Linda has worked hard to recover from her overwhelming anxiety from which she has suffered ever since Nicolaj's birth. She can control her anxiety without medication today, but must always be mindful not to become too stressed. Although Linda has worked part time since Nicolaj's birth, a constant and almost hopeless economic situation is the price she pays for her choice. Until a few months ago, despite her lack of support from family or friends, and Nikolaj's chronic health problems, Linda successfully remained in the labour market. Most recently, however, Linda has been unemployed and is hoping to find a new part-time clerical job, but the competition is stiff and she has been forced to return to full unemployment benefits.

Who will help Linda cope with her acute anxieties and her intense attachment to her son? While Linda received support from the private social worker at Boligfonden and from the child psychologist who evaluated Nicolaj when he was an infant, she has since lost faith in the health visitor who she feels let her down at a crucial meeting when Nikolaj attended the infant centre. Hence Linda's general mistrust of the public system will probably make it hard for her to ask for further help in the future or to find what she feels she needs – "a grown-up, motherly person" at her side. Who is going to help Linda re-enter the labour market again? The longer she is out of work, the harder it will be for her to re-enter as a lone mother. Having a job is important to Linda's self-esteem, even if, up until now, she has not benefited economically from working. Such are Linda's ongoing economic and psychological obstacles as she struggles to survive on her own, with only Nicolaj and anxiety as her constant companions.

Mona and Dennis

"Every time they find a new disease with Dennis, they say that it has become chronic. It is still the same with his ears. He is now going to the hospital for an operation where a muscle around his ear has to be shortened in order to close his ear drum. It has not been closed the last 18 months, and there is a risk of becoming deaf if it is not closed. He continues to get ear infections, and every time a drain is put in, the ear itself pushes it out again.... Sometimes I have to clean up pus which has dripped out of his ear onto the floor. He has taken stronger and stronger antibiotics, but now the bacteria is resistant to antibiotics."

Before Dennis was born, Mona lived with his father for eight years while she worked as a home help assistant[3]. Her pregnancy with Dennis was a very difficult time – she broke up with Dennis' father and also contracted rubella. People close to Mona pressured her to have an abortion because of the possible dangers rubella posed for her unborn child. But Mona, who had already undergone two earlier abortions, very much wanted to continue this pregnancy. Although Mona liked her job as a home help assistant and was proud of having missed only two days of work in the eight years she had been employed, she was not able to return to work after her maternity leave because the job was too physically demanding, and because of Dennis' chronic health problems. Since his birth, Mona has had to fight for adequate housing that will not further damage Dennis' fragile health.

Mona and Dennis – the stress of the early years

Mona and Dennis' first days together in the hospital were confusing and painful for Mona. Because of the uncertainty about fetal damage to Dennis and the risk of infection from the rubella she had contracted while pregnant, they were isolated from all the other mothers and babies in the hospital. Mona remembers:

> "It was a terrible time. He would not take my breast. The nurses were all so busy, and they forgot to put him to my breast. It was my first baby, and I did not know anything about how to breastfeed Dennis. He would not drink, and every time I tried to feed him one of the nurses pressed my breast, and another nurse gave me a feeding bottle, and a third nurse took away the feeding bottle again. They disagreed about everything, and that was one of the worst things for me.... I don't know if he could feel all this insecurity around him.... It was really terrible, and since then he has eaten very little."

Five days after the birth, Mona and Dennis were sent home from the hospital to a flat that was damp and without heat or hot water. Although doctors found no indication of fetal damage from rubella, Dennis soon developed ear infections. After some months, Mona was assigned another flat with a gas stove for better heat. However, the stove soon malfunctioned and central heating was installed. Even with these improvements the windows in her second flat were in extremely bad condition – the window sills let in so much outside air that they "could be used as a refrigerator". Soon Dennis also suffered from eczema and bronchial asthma, the latter accompanied by intense coughing spells at night. He had persistent eating problems and also wet his bed regularly, sometimes three or four times a night. Dennis' doctor stated that Mona and Dennis needed a better flat and that Dennis' health would not improve until the draughty and cold conditions were improved upon.

When Mona asked the social centre for help in finding a modern flat, the social centre ignored the doctor's recommendation. Staff told Mona that moving to a modern flat was impossible. She was told that she was not entitled to raise her housing expenditures while she was living on social assistance. As time passed and Dennis' health problems worsened, Mona became desperate and determined to act to change her living situation. Finally, she managed to find a modern flat through a cooperative housing organization, and she obtained a public housing deposit. The social welfare centre reacted immediately to the news that Mona had found herself a new flat. They denied Mona any money for her moving expenses, and they said that she could not expect help with her first month's rent. Mona contacted the private organization Boligfonden and asked for help. Through Boligfonden, Mona got the necessary economic support for her moving expenses and her first month's rent.

Mona's social network and her struggle for an education

Dennis' many health problems demanded a lot of work and effort from Mona, often 24 hours a day. Because Mona wanted to take care of her fragile son herself, Dennis did not start day care until he was five years old and Mona lived on social assistance during these years. Besides the help she received from Boligfonden, Mona and Dennis have a close relationship with Dennis' paternal grandmother, who is in touch with them daily. She has given Mona a lot of practical and personal support, and Dennis calls her every night before bedtime to say good night. Dennis' father is seriously sick with diabetes, yet he keeps in close contact with Dennis. Mona has had no contact with her own family for many years, after earlier conflicts in her relationship with them. The pedagogues at Dennis' day care and the teachers at school-age child care have also been important people in the lives of Mona and Dennis. Mona has always had a good relationship with them and feels they have given her much support.

When Dennis started day care, Mona wanted to improve her education, to get back into the workforce, and to break her dependence on social assistance by studying to become a pedagogue. The social centre, however, resisted her plans and told her that because she had been able to support herself as a home help assistant for the eight years before Dennis was born, they would now have difficulty getting educational support for her through §43 (see Chapter 1, Note 2). Mona told the social centre staff about her inability to work again as a home help assistant and also that the job was too physically demanding for her. She said that sometimes she had feelings of paralysis in her arms, for instance when she carried Dennis as a baby. Even though Mona repeatedly explained that these health problems made it impossible for her to return to work as a home help assistant, she could not get a clear answer about her eligibility for §43 support.

Once again, Mona determinedly tried to find a way to resolve her problem. She decided to start going to school while continuing to live on her general social assistance allowance. In practice, this proved to be almost impossible for her. She enrolled in a one-year HF course[4] taught in the evenings and arranged for Dennis' grandmother to babysit while she attended her course. This proved to be difficult because Dennis, after having been in day care all day, reacted negatively when Mona left him three evenings a week to attend school. A very supportive teacher persuaded Mona not to give up and told her that she had good skills. Mona began again, this time at a slower pace, in a two-year course that offered classes during the day. Even though she was denied §43 support and Dennis' fragile health caused a lot of absences from her classes, with determination and support from Dennis' grandmother, her teacher, and the after-school day care pedagogues, Mona has been able to complete this two-year course.

Dennis today at 10 years old

"We have been closely related to each other after having been constantly together for the first five years [of Dennis' life]. It has been most difficult for me to loosen our relationship.... But he is moving away from me more and more and that is OK ... and I have become better at letting him go.... I have signed a note giving him permission to climb the 16 meter wall and so on.... He is a ... playful child, and I try and let him be a child as long as possible.... He is good at playing with other children of all ages."

Mona says that Dennis is fond of his small private school for children of lone mothers. He is good at reading, English, and mathematics, although he does not like the latter: "He rings the doorbell at home and asks me if I will do his homework for him. He says he will pay me with his pocket money!" Since Mona and Dennis moved to their new flat two years ago, there have been some improvements in his health. Although his ear infections have grown chronic, Dennis' bronchial asthma has almost disappeared. He is still extremely sensitive to cold and moisture; if he is out in rainy weather, he begins to cough almost immediately. His bedwetting has significantly decreased after he received some zone therapy. At 10 years old, Dennis' weight is only 23 kilos, and Mona says that it has been an ongoing struggle to get Dennis to eat. She spends a lot of money for various natural health supplements added to his food. Because of his many illnesses, Dennis' motor development is delayed and he has difficulty keeping up with activities like other children his own age.

"He was always the last one when running with his friends ... but today it is much better, and he swings himself in the climbing frame. His gym teacher says that he looks like a small and fragile boy who needs to be looked after carefully, but in reality he is the child who is working the hardest."

The future for Mona and Dennis

Mona's experiences with the public social welfare system have been anything but positive. She has had to fight for every improvement in her living conditions and says that it was difficult to find someone who would meet and talk with her personally about her situation. There has been endless turnover in social work staff at the social centre, and she has often been told "it is not for me to decide; this is a decision for someone else in our system". Dennis' serious and ongoing health problems were ignored by the social centre in relation to Mona and Dennis' desperate housing situation. Even when she succeeded in finding a better flat for herself, Mona experienced retribution from the social centre instead of support. Were it not for Mona's determination and the help she received from Boligfonden, their living conditions and Dennis' health problems would undoubtedly be much worse than they are today. Mona has also waged a long fight against the social centre about her eligibility for §43 educational support. Determined to improve her education and secure a good job, Mona sought and received help from Dennis' grandmother, his after-school day care pedagogues, and from her own teacher. At this point, Mona has completed the first year of her studies to become a pedagogue and finally, after a protracted struggle, has been approved for §43 educational support. Mona reports that she is very fond of her studies, even though she is the oldest student in her class. Mona's determination and persistence appear finally to have paid off, as she sets her sights on her goal of completing her post-secondary education and becoming a professional pedagogue in the near future. Mona fervently aspires to be economically self-sufficient and to terminate her dependence on social assistance. As a lone mother who has overcome many obstacles for herself and her son, she has also had to contend with punitive actions by the staff at the social centre, who have placed continuous roadblocks on her path to independence through education.

The struggle to survive as a family

As we consider the complex and traumatic lives of Hanne, Gina, Linda, and Mona and the scarred childhoods of their children, a clearer picture of the multiple obstacles they have encountered begins to emerge. Whether they receive income from low-paid work, unemployment benefits, or social assistance, we see that they and their children have experienced more traumatic events than most, and lived with far higher levels of stress, ranging from abusive childhoods and domestic violence, to sick children and substandard housing. And these private crises, persisting for years, have often been met by an increasingly restrictive and inflexible level of economic support from the public social assistance system, a situation which contributes to an even greater risk of turbulence and despair due to their stretched family budgets. Clearly for many of the mothers, the path out of poverty to a viable family life is through education, which brings higher earning potential and the promise of future stability. In the following chapter, the lives of Jette and Ditte are chronicled –

two lone mothers who, like Mona, have had to fight for their rights to an education.

Notes

[1] A weekend family is an official relief family that serves as a supplementary foster family on weekends for a child who is considered vulnerable and in need of stable mature parental role models. Often such a family will form close bonds with the child and parent over an extended period of time. The child may spend every weekend or one weekend a month with the weekend family, frequently providing relief for a stressed lone mother.

[2] A health visitor is a visiting nurse with paediatric post-graduate training who makes home visits and offers medical advice and services as well as emotional support and practical child-rearing advice to parents.

[3] A home help assistant (*hjemmehjælper*) is a social and health service assistant, a paraprofessional who makes home visits and takes care of food preparation, personal toiletries/washing, and house cleaning in private homes (mostly for disabled, elderly and vulnerable individuals).

[4] General Upper Secondary Education in Denmark has two tracks: the 'Gymnasium' and the 'Higher Preparatory Examination' (HF). Both qualify students for admission to university and higher education studies. The three-year long Gymnasium is (mostly) attended by young students in direct continuation of the 10th year of the Folkschool. The HF has a high number of adults who have left the education system and wish to return. The HF can be completed in two years of full-time study, but for adults the examination can also be taken on a single-subject basis or subject combinations extended over a longer period of time.

FOUR

Fighting for an education

Jette and Ditte are young lone mothers who have experienced difficult and stressful life events placing them outside the labour market for several years. While each has received some short-term vocational education, they are determined to pursue post-secondary education and professional careers that will enable them to earn a viable family income and become economically independent. They both see education as a crucial resource that will empower them to take control over their lives, thereby providing a different future for themselves and their children. Jette and Ditte have recently been refused rehabilitation educational assistance (§43) from their social centres, and both have experienced serious personal doubts, the refusals producing in them strong feelings "of being nothing". As an extra humiliation, each was told by the social centre to think about taking short-term courses to prepare to be paraprofessional workers in the health care system, jobs which would essentially consign them to low-wage employment.

Several of the mothers in our study have related similar stories of refusals for §43 assistance for their educational plans. In each case the only educational offer was a one-year basic training programme as a paraprofessional within the health care system. This type of education appears to have been categorized (and stereotypically so) as appropriate and sufficient for lone mothers, reflecting patriarchal thinking about the function and placement of women within the labour market. For lone mothers such as Jette and Ditte, who are the sole providers for their young children, the wages paid for paraprofessional 'pink collar', 'feminized' jobs are simply too low to make ends meet.

Jette and Morten

"[After the accident] I broke down and I couldn't see anything ... I felt so bad ... so I went to the doctor and said I could not manage ... I only thought of sleeping all the time.... But I have this loan now and then I have to take new loans and I don't know what next ... and I think I am in a really tough situation, but I don't understand why they [the social welfare authorities] don't help me."

Jette (26 years old) and her four-year-old son, Morten, are currently living in a large communal house with other single parents and their children. The house specifically caters to the needs of single parents who are enrolled in higher education, and is funded by the private Boligfonden organization in Copenhagen. Jette, who has some vocational training, is currently receiving unemployment benefits, and has now decided she wants to become a nurse. Jette's partner, Bo, was killed in a car accident several months prior to our first interview, and she and Morten are struggling to survive the loss and the shock of the tragedy. Jette's ongoing concerns about Morten's reaction to his father's death and his developmental needs are interwoven with her own anxieties about her capacity to cope. For Jette, who vacillates between extreme feelings of despair and aspirations towards building a new future for herself and Morten, there are several key obstacles she has encountered that relate to severe economic hardship, the lack of supportive services from the social welfare centre, and continuing frustrations and roadblocks related to her educational aspirations. Vital to her capacity to continue to endure has been the supportive social network at the Boligfonden house, and the responsive interventions from a social worker at the private Boligfonden agency.

Confronting the tragedy

"Morten and I were at a skiing holiday in Italy with some of our friends. And when we came home, we got the message ... it happened the same morning ... he was in a bad accident. He was under the car ... I couldn't bear to think of him lying there, my husband, totally alone, but I didn't want to remember him as a corpse ... [so] I decided not to see him."

Jette describes the immediate aftermath of the accident and dealing with Bo's mother and grandparents:

"Oh, it has been hard ... we help each other, but they had a really hard time. His mother – he was her only child and she was feeling really bad and she, in the first place ... she neglected that we had been living together for four years, [she acted as if] she knew him better ... she said, 'I have lost – I have lost my only child – it's worse than you losing your husband because you are so young and you can go out and find a new man'. And perhaps she is right, it's harder to lose a child, but this [is now the reality of the] situation, we are standing here ... and it doesn't help ... it was really bad at that time.... I was very alone and I needed him so much.... It was really hard for me because I ran all around just to get some help, because I felt so bad."

Jette struggled to find a psychologist who could help her cope, but she received no help from the social centre. In desperation she went to the hospital's crisis centre with Bo's mother, but Jette encountered further problems when she and Bo's mother found themselves placed with "two idiots" who were no help at all. Jette finally managed to obtain a referral to a psychologist, and she also received an anti-depressant medication from her doctor. What is significant in Jette's account is the series of obstacles and bureaucratic delays she was forced to endure while in shock. She was particularly concerned about her ability to cope with her son who, at the time of the accident, was only two-and-a-half years old. At Morten's day care centre, Jette was more successful in accessing assistance and was able to depend on the psychologist there who offered her advice about how to break the news to him:

"He didn't know where his father was. I told him he was dead and up in heaven and he tried a lot of times to reach him ... he said if he had a very long wooden stick, he could reach up and get him down again ... [and I told him] we couldn't get him down because you had to die first to get where he was, and we didn't want that ... we should live our lives, and he should grow up ... and then he thought when he grows up and becomes a father and he gets a child ... then [is] he going to die? I said 'No – that's not the right way' ... and then he took this long wooden stick and he tried to get him down again ... and he said, 'Well if I can't get father back, I want a new one'."

Jette and Morten: the struggle to rebuild their lives

Jette described how Morten initially became very aggressive towards other children at the day care centre and she blamed herself for her emotional absence, and her inability to cope with her depression. "I think perhaps it was because I was all the time ... not there for him ... and if he had a problem with the other children [at the day care centre] he didn't know he could come to me ... [because he thought] 'Of course mother is feeling bad, so I just hit them'."

After Jette obtained medication from her doctor, who she feels has been supportive, she describes gradually overcoming her depression and suicidal feelings, and becoming more able to be responsive to Morten, who, she says, during this period, changed from "always a happy child to being sad all the time". When Morten turned three and moved from the infant day care centre, the pedagogues at the new centre were very concerned about his cognitive development and urged Jette to consult a psychologist. However, the problem appeared to be related to his eyesight, and after the doctor prescribed glasses, Morten changed quite dramatically and now appears to be adjusting well.

Jette describes Morten as a shy child who needs time to get to know people, but once he opens up, he makes friends rather easily. Jette states that since she has begun to recover, she and Morten "have fun together" and Morten has many playmates at the day care centre and at the Boligfonden house. Jette is often concerned that Morten wants friends so badly that he puts up with a lot of teasing and doesn't react to many situations when he is provoked. She continues to experience many conflicting emotions regarding her own feelings: she has had qualms about letting go of Morten at day care; at the same time, she wants him to develop his own sense of autonomy.

> "He is very happy at the day care but sometimes he doesn't want to go there and he wants to stay home with me ... sometimes it's hard for him to say good-bye in the mornings ... but when he starts playing, it goes all right ... maybe he is afraid that something may happen to me ... he says he'd rather stay home with me ... he is very attached to me but I'm probably more attached to him!"

Jette is insightful about her own attachment needs and continually links her own struggle to overcome her grief with Morten's development, and says that she has tried to be as honest as possible with Morten about the death of his father. Morten still refuses to go to the cemetery, "It's as if he is afraid that I will be upset again", and she feels that Morten hides his emotions. However, Jette feels that generally he has adjusted, although she worries about her own ongoing capacity to cope:

"Sometimes I'm doing well but I keep falling into these deep holes –
I become so tired and depressed as if everything falls apart.... I spend
a lot of time just keeping myself above water. I think a lot about
Bo.... If I'm doing OK and everything is all right, I can see Morten is
very happy [at the day care] ... he tells me many things and if he is
feeling very confident, he also tells me when he has been naughty."

Morten's daily world

Several observations at Morten's day care centre and conversations
with his pedagogue reveal that Morten is a shy, but resilient child
who has adapted well to the social world of day care, which he has
attended for about two years. When he first enrolled, shortly after
the accident, he talked a lot about his father, but his focus on his
father has diminished over time. The pedagogue confirms that while
Morten is quiet and often appears passive, he does interact and play
sociably with other children, although he rarely takes the initiative
in group play, preferring to participate rather than lead. Since his
vision problem has been corrected, his interests and play have changed
dramatically. He now loves to draw and do puzzles, and will stay
intensely focused on one activity for long periods of time. During
the previous year, the pedagogue had noticed Morten behaving
aggressively when Jette came to pick him up, almost as if "he could
tell Jette was not feeling well and Morten reacted to that. He was
just feeling so good in the day care and then mom came feeling
depressed and he didn't want to go home with her". The pedagogue
and Jette discussed this behaviour and she suggested that Jette try
and set some limits and that she should not feel so sorry for Morten.
The pedagogue describes how much better Morten is doing now
since Jette has become stronger, and describes Morten as "a charming
boy who lately has started to have fun", and participates far more
actively in the day care. However, the pedagogue, like Jette, expresses
concerns about Morten's lack of assertiveness as he will put up with
a lot from other children in order to please them.

The following observation of Morten at his day care centre in the
spring of 1997 reveals a quiet, self-contained, child who has adjusted
well to his peers, and is actively engaged in play:

Morten is very involved in a long conversation with the pedagogue
when I arrive – he is very engaged in his play but does not talk much

and appears to be a rather quiet boy. Morten goes off with another boy and the pedagogue to wash some toys in the bathroom. He is very busy and eagerly follows the pedagogue's directions. When he and the other child disagree about which toys to wash, Morten makes his opinion known quietly without a fight. While he washes a toy animal, he takes it apart and puts it back together again – working in a very focused manner with a long concentration span. When he is finished he goes to the table to wait for snacks, but soon gets up and fetches a puzzle from the shelf and works at it while waiting for the other children to finish cleaning up. When I initiate conversation with him, he is reserved, but later shows me his puzzles. He invents a name, 'Rasmus', as part of his fantasy play and tells me that's his name. When his mother comes to pick him up he ignores her and she sits watching him for about five minutes. At first he does not react when she speaks to him but then begins a conversation with her without looking up. When she tells him she is leaving for a short time to talk with the pedagogue he again does not react, but continues to be engaged in his play.

Six months later Morten is observed again at the same centre:

When I arrive the children are outside in the playground, and Morten is in the sandbox with another child, Peter. He is very aware as I watch him, as the two boys engage in imaginative play – the sand becomes cement and they are house builders. Morten: "You can use clay but it shouldn't be wet 'cos it doesn't look good when it's supposed to be a house – don't you think?" Peter asks: "Should the house be that big?" [showing with his hands]. Morten and Peter take turns digging and busily stirring the sand in the bucket, muttering, "We don't want an ugly house". After Morten throws water at Peter, he says, "Don't! Do you think it's funny having water thrown at you?" Morten responds: "Out in the water when there are waves" – and the conflict defuses and they begin to talk about swimming in the sea in the summertime. Morten is actively engaged while there are just two of them playing, however, when an older boy, Paul, joins them and takes some of his clay, Morten responds, saying: "You shouldn't always take my clay". After Morten repeats this twice, and Paul continues and says "No", Morten runs away and begins to play alone, complaining that the other boys keep taking his clay, but they ignore him. After the boys call him back, he returns a few minutes later and soon a conflict ensues over ownership of sand boxes – the boys begin to throw sand at Morten and he angrily kicks their sand buildings down and throws sand back at them. At that point a fruit snack is served, and Morten leaves and goes to tell the pedagogue that Paul threw sand at him, but she does not pay any attention. During the snack Morten again quietly seeks attention but does not succeed and talks to himself, saying, "It was me who did it ... but something happened to my glasses". He continues until one of the pedagogues finally responds and takes his glasses and washes them.

During these observations of Morten, it is clear that while he initially withdraws from conflict, he has also learned to assert himself and reacts aggressively when his play is interrupted by other children. However, because he is generally rather quiet and reserved, he is often not heard by the pedagogues, yet he is also persistent and continues with a quiet determination until he is acknowledged. During the two-year period in the day care centre, Morten has shown a great deal of progress, is learning to assert himself, and has developed confidence in his relationships with adults and with children.

Being alone and the vital role of a supportive network

Jette talks of her sudden new life as a lone mother as "being very hard", so that, "I just want[ed] to scream". Initially, after the accident, she felt very alone and isolated. Her parents divorced when she was a child, and her relationship with them is tenuous; she has only a distant relationship with her mother and has not spoken to her father for six years. She is far closer to Bo's mother and grandparents with whom she stayed for two months after the tragedy. She feels she can depend on them for some child care assistance with Morten, if she needs it. However, the most significant network she has found is through the Boligfonden house and the collective life she shares with the other lone parents, all of whom are studying and taking care of their children. In addition, she has received strong support from one of the social workers at Boligfonden, who helped her initially, has supported her emotionally and advocated on her behalf at the social centre. As Jette reflected on her experiences, she remarked that in the beginning, "I felt so alone", but that changed after moving into the house:

"I got a lot of support in this house ... they are really sweet ... all the time we do things for each other ... and if you're broke then your neighbour says, 'Come and eat with me this evening' ... we sort of take care of each other and help each other ... it's really nice ... we manage well here.... I think it [the network support] is very important ... because none of us could imagine how to live [alone] in our own flats."

Confronting the obstacles: housing, economic difficulties, and §43 refusal

After Bo's death, Jette faced severe economic hardship. She was left with many debts to pay from Bo, who she described as "a pretty wild person". When he was killed, they were staying at a summer house and as it was very isolated, and as she no longer had a car, she was desperate: "Our economy [financial situation] was bad and I didn't know what to do with myself". She initially stayed with Bo's mother and grandparents and through the advice of a lawyer friend, contacted Boligfonden Housing Foundation and was allocated a small flat in their communal house. She is extremely appreciative of all the support she received from the social workers at that private agency, in contrast to the indifferent treatment she feels she has received from the public system's social centre (which paid moving expenses of 7,000 Dkr, but provided no other assistance). Jette receives unemployment benefits and although the rent at her small flat is very low – 1,820 Dkr a month (for a one-room flat and free maintenance and use of facilities such as laundry) – Jette still has a difficult time balancing a tight budget, which includes about 600 Dkr a month for day care costs as well as debt payments, transport, clothes and union dues. After her monthly costs are paid, which total about 6,000 Dkr, Jette is left with just 1,000 Dkr per month to pay her loans and living costs.

Jette's severe economic situation has been exacerbated by the social centre's refusal to approve her application under §43 for a nursing degree. She already had a limited business education, but requested approval for rehabilitation and she applied to, and was accepted at, nursing school. However, her application for §43 was denied; she was told that the working hours were too difficult for a lone mother, and that she would be over-classified in comparison to her previous educational situation; instead she was offered a one-year lower-level home help training. Jette appealed against the decision, but she was once again refused. This created further stress for Jette:

"They thought I should only get the one-year home help training ... but I always wanted to be a nurse ... and I think it's very important that when I'm alone now, that this education, will bring me something ... and I want more responsibility in the job ... but they thought I will be over-classified in comparison with my situation before ... and they said that my situation as a lone mother would make it too hard for me with the changing working hours and that was their reason [for refusal] ... but we found out that it is not the case ... and the social worker at Boligfonden found out it is not a problem for a nurse now to get day hours.... But I think this [refusal] is very hard and I just want to scream ... and I don't know where on earth I can go ... I think I'm in a tough situation and I don't understand why they don't help."

Jette describes how upset she was when the social worker at the social centre started questioning her about why she wanted to be a nurse, instead of a home help assistant!

"I felt really bad when I was there ... I was really vulnerable, so I said help me ... but he didn't want to.... If you sometimes have your own idea yourself, if you're having some needs ... [and] they want to give you something [else] and you say no to this offer, they think – oh, you are so spoiled, like you have to be happy for what you are offered."

After the appeal was refused, Jette, angry and frustrated, decided to enrol in nursing school anyway, by taking out an additional loan which has created new debts and further economic hardship. While Jette anticipated that she would have to survive on SU (see Chapter 2, Note 1), she recently heard that she was eligible to receive further unemployment compensation for two years from the unemployment benefit system. This unemployment assistance is higher than the SU payments, which makes Jette's economic situation far more viable. SU is completely inadequate for a lone mother and child to live on, and no additional payments are made when students, such as Jette, have children to support (see Appendix B).

Jette, Morten and the future

Jette has not received adequate or appropriate support from her social centre. She has been treated indifferently by the social authorities, and has had to fight for whatever minimal financial help she has received. On the other hand, the public day care system has been a strong source of support for Morten and, for a child coping with the death of his father and the emotional depression of his mother, the day care has provided an alternative healthy social world for Morten. The pedagogues have intervened sensitively and have offered helpful advice to Jette at critical times in the past year. The private housing agency, Boligfonden, has served as another pillar of support and advocacy for Jette, and encouraged her to pursue a professional degree, as opposed to the low-level training offered by the social centre. Lone mothers such as Jette often find themselves caught in a 'Catch-22' – if Jette were to accept the low-level training offered by the social centre, she would remain in debt and be condemned to the bottom rungs of a low-wage economy, unable to improve her family status and adequately care for her child in the future. If, on the other hand, she chooses to follow her educational aspirations, she saddles herself with burdensome debts (even with the increased payments from unemployment benefits) which increase her economic vulnerability should one element of this carefully stacked deck overturn. Yet, to Jette, becoming a nurse offers a vision of a viable future – even though the risks involved place her and Morten in a precarious economic situation. It is clear that the coming years will demand enormous resilience and coping strategies from a vulnerable mother and child who are still traumatized by loss and tragedy. A central question that emerges from the case of Jette and Morten is why should this young family, perched precariously between economic self-sufficiency or dependency, not receive adequate economic support through §43? Do the new policies which diminish the importance of education and instead emphasize work activation serve the long-term interests of lone mothers and their children? Clearly future family stability depends on the opportunity to enter the labour market on a strong footing, and professional education is a clear path out of poverty, high debts, and continuing low wages.

Ditte and Julia

"The social system ... gives me the message that I am worth nothing at all."

Twenty-five-year-old Ditte is struggling to build a viable future for herself and her two-year-old daughter, Julia. Leaving school after 10th grade and her parents' home when she was 17, Ditte has supported herself in her own flat by working several unskilled jobs, the last in a chemical factory. A short time after she met Julia's father, Ditte gave up her own flat and moved in with him. He was anxious for them to have a child together, but Ditte had some doubts about their relationship. After just two-and-a-half weeks of living together, Julia's father suddenly asked Ditte to move out. Left without a home, Ditte realized that she was pregnant. She also quit her job at the factory fearing possible toxic effects from the chemicals there. With the help of a friend, Ditte was able to find a flat at Egmontgården during the fourth month of her pregnancy. Since that time, she has faced obstacles such as depression, economic hardship, and despair at the thwarting of her hopes to leave the unskilled workforce and complete a three-year educational programme to become a technical assistant, a career she feels will help secure her future and Julia's.

Struggling through a desperate situation

With her pregnancy came a very difficult period for Ditte. Many people advised her to get an abortion, but Ditte felt that this was impossible for her. She felt that, in a way, her baby was planned, and she could only choose to keep it, saying, "I wouldn't have an abortion. I had tried that before, and I couldn't take it". Ditte did not know what to do – she was depressed, sick, and wanted to sleep all the time; her situation felt desperate, she did not know where to turn to for help, and she had no place to live. After looking through the telephone directory with a girlfriend, Ditte telephoned the Boligfonden Foundation and they suggested that she contact Egmontgården, where she was immediately offered a flat. Ditte describes how relieved she was on finding the flat: "I had been very sick in the other town. The same day I moved in [at Egmontgården], all my worries stopped".

After Julia's birth Ditte stayed in the hospital for five days where the only help she received from the nurses was how to breastfeed her new baby. To her surprise, none of the doctors or nurses asked Ditte about her situation, even though she says they must have noticed that there were no visits from her child's father. "And there wasn't anyone who asked me if there was help for me when I leave the hospital, nothing". What would have been better, says Ditte, is "a doctor who sits down and talks to you and tells you something instead of just saying good-bye". Ditte would have liked better preparation and support from the hospital before coming home alone with her baby. She wonders, with an ironic smile, "Maybe this is the way Denmark hopes to make lone mothers stronger".

The first week home with Julia was Ditte's most difficult period, as she felt vulnerable and alone, and the sudden change to being a new mother "was a shock":

> "I tried to be the best mother in the world for her, so I forgot about taking care of myself. I forgot to eat, and I got sick. I couldn't stand on my feet at all. My father called me and asked how things were going, and I couldn't lie anymore. He came with food and everything and helped me, and he has come very often ever since."

Although Ditte's former partner has virtually abandoned his daughter, Ditte has tried to stay in contact with him for Julia's sake: "I think she has a right to have a father". Julia's father now lives with another woman and has recently been in court fighting for custody of a son from an earlier relationship, and has explicitly told Ditte that his son comes before Julia. He claims he is very ill and that he will die within the next two years, although Ditte does not know whether or not to believe him "because he has done so many things to me". All in all Julia's father has seen his daughter only three times in her young life, and Ditte finds it very upsetting that he is indifferent towards Julia: "That has been difficult ... because I love her so much that I can't understand why he doesn't love her too".

Networks of support

Ditte's current support network is comprised of Egmontgården and her father, with whom she has developed a close relationship since Julia's birth. She is not on good terms with her mother, and her relationships with her friends have changed since Julia was born:

"We have very different lifestyles now, but I try keeping in touch with some of them. But I think I can read something in their eyes, maybe a little bit of pity [for me].... When I tell them I lived at the Lone Mothers' House [Egmontgården], they are really surprised ... so sometimes when they ask me where I live, I just answer Østerbro. Some months ago I had a boyfriend, but he wanted to take a strong father role with Julia, and I was not prepared for that at all."

Ditte describes Egmontgården as a place where she enjoyed a support network, and she expresses anxiety about losing this help when she moves into her new flat:

"The Lone Mothers' House has been the perfect place for me.... You get the support services all in one place.... In the evenings when our children are sleeping, we sometimes drink coffee together, and we leave our doors open so we can listen if the babies cry.... It has been relaxing [to live] here but also hard.... They are very nice here, but they can't help with everything.... [In my new flat] I think I will be more alone. It might be hard in the beginning.... The one thing I fear is if Julia becomes sick. I will not be able to just go next door and say, 'Would you look at this? Have you seen this before?'... I'm used to people [at Egmontgården] helping me all the time, and I can help them, and then suddenly I will be alone.... I'm afraid I will be a little bit lonely.... But after that, I think I will really like it because [in my new flat] there won't always be someone knocking at the door saying hello. I have now been offered a flat through the municipal housing system. It is a cheap and good flat. I don't think they will give me something better, so I have to say yes now."

The social workers at Egmontgården have been especially supportive of Ditte, helping her adjust to her new life with Julia and constantly encouraging her to pursue her educational plans. With their help, Ditte has joined a mothers' group which is guided by a health visitor (visiting paediatric nurse). Ditte explains why she sought a mothers' group outside of Egmontgården:

"I wouldn't be with anyone here in the [Lone Mothers'] House because I want to see how other people live ... a real family. [In my mothers' group] I won't always talk about being alone and how hard it is and about why a man is leaving me. I want to think about other things and talk about other things."

Besides her participation in the mothers' group and the ongoing help of her own father, the health visitor is also a key source of support for Ditte.

Ditte and Julia: a close relationship

According to Ditte, Julia's family day care home provider described her as a bright child. Julia walked early and said the numbers 1-2-3 when she was 10 months old, which surprised the health visitor. She sleeps well, from 7.00 pm until the next morning, and appears to be a happy and sociable child who is very demanding of Ditte's attention, often displaying a fighting spirit and strong temper. Ditte is concerned that Julia is far more demanding than other children her age. She thinks that this is because they have been inseparable ever since Julia's birth, and Julia has become accustomed to the intense contact with her. Ditte comments, "It can be a little hard on me". For a period during Julia's first year, their intense relationship caused a real crisis for Ditte because of Julia's excessive and constant demand for her attention. If Julia were left alone for a moment, such as when Ditte went to open a window or to use the bathroom, Julia would start screaming at once, and she reacted with constant crying to any changes in routine. Ditte felt overwhelmed, and in her desperation asked the health visitor for advice. Ditte says, "The umbilical cord had not been cut", and she believed that they were too close to one another: "I didn't have anything else in my life ... I was at home with Julia all day long, and I didn't have a man.... Therefore we established this relationship". The health visitor helped Ditte set some limits for Julia and create a more relaxed and balanced pattern of interactions. Today, Ditte feels that the relationship is "normal", and she describes Julia as:

> "... exploring limits like other children, maybe a little sensitive. Julia has difficulties amusing herself, she likes attention.... She is not hyperactive, but curious and likes to be stimulated.... She cannot sit playing by herself for a longer period of time like other children."

Initially the family day care home was a good choice for both Julia and Ditte. Julia was happy to go there in the morning, and this was an enormous relief to Ditte, allowing her to feel that she had more energy and helping her to develop a healthier relationship with her daughter. However, after several months, when Julia was 20 months old, Ditte explains that "the chemistry" between the family day care provider and Julia went wrong, and the provider eventually found it unbearable to take care of Julia because she cried so much. Consequently, Ditte moved Julia to a day care centre, and is pleased with the change and thinks Julia is much happier. The pedagogue describes Julia as a well-developed sociable child who is easy to comfort, although she has a strong temper, and the very first time at the day care she demonstrated this by lying on the floor and screaming loudly each time she did not get what she wanted. But this pattern has been broken and she has now adjusted well to her day care world.

Fighting for an education: economic hardship and §43 refusal

During her late adolescence and early adult years, Ditte had four or five different unskilled jobs, each between 6 and 18 months long. She found the jobs herself and has often been asked to come back to some of the same worksites. She worked in a supermarket but left when the job was extended to cleaning bathrooms often used by drug abusers; she enrolled in a six-month period of job training in food preparation for a nursery; she worked in a firm producing bijouterie; and she worked in a chemical factory, but quit when she became pregnant as she worried about the ill-effects the chemicals may have on her unborn child. Ditte's aspirations for a viable future with a decent salary led her to recognize that she needed to move beyond low-wage unskilled dead-end jobs if she was going to be a good provider for her small family; hence she decided to enrol in a three-year professional educational programme to become a technical assistant.

When Ditte applied for §43 support to continue her education and become a technical assistant, her application was refused. The reason the social centre gave was, "You have earlier been employed in the unskilled working area and there should be no hindrances for you to continue working in this area" (excerpt from the social centre letter of refusal, 10 July 1996).

Ditte was both astonished and angered by this refusal because she had been under the impression from meetings with her social workers that she would receive §43 support and be able to pursue her educational plans. Ditte felt that the social centre's letter of refusal sent a message to her that she was "worth nothing at all", consigning her to the lowest paid, physically demanding jobs which keep her on the margins of life. According to Ditte's record at the social centre, she must demonstrate a "deadlock situation in relation to the labour market which shall be proved before §43 support can be given". On the other hand, with a professional technical education, she would earn a higher salary and be a good role model for Julia, ensuring that as a lone mother she would be able to secure her future and that of her child.

After Ditte appealed against the first refusal of educational support, and after she had received yet another refusal, Ditte's "whole world broke down", and she was in despair. The social workers at Egmontgården had written a recommendation letter to the social centre on Ditte's behalf, but to no avail. However, at the social centre, a concerned social worker who had helped Ditte file her appeals encouraged her to enrol at the Technical School despite the denial of her request for §43 support. Ditte has since decided to start her programme at the Technical School, using the minimal SU grant amount and taking out maximum loans, in order to survive on a very stretched budget with Julia. Ditte talks about her hopes and her determination: "When I got Julia, I got some kind of energy which I never had before. This energy is mobilized when I am fighting and being rejected. I cannot promise myself that I will accomplish the education, but I will try".

Ditte's daily life now runs according to a very tight time schedule: she attends school until 3.00 pm, then picks up Julia from day care, does housework and shopping, and studies at night. "But", says Ditte, "if you manage your life well, then you have to work hard".

The future for Ditte and Julia

Ditte's experiences as a young and vulnerable lone mother are telling. Clearly the supportive network at Egmontgården helped her begin her life as a young mother with her new-born daughter. Now Ditte is determined to provide economically for herself and for Julia, but she has been refused appropriate social system support for an education that would help ensure a promising and secure future. The refusal by the social centre to provide Ditte with §43 support demonstrates the counterproductive practices that perpetuate poverty and deny opportunities to lone mothers for post-secondary education and access to higher paying jobs, which would provide a path out of dependence on the social system. As a result of the §43 refusal, Ditte now feels humiliated by the social system and has started to finance her own education. Pursuing an education on her own while she is solely responsible for her young daughter creates an extremely difficult economic situation for Ditte. Living on the minimal SU monthly amount is impossible because it is not regulated for family size. And like other lone mothers, Ditte finds she cannot supplement her SU grant by working part time, because she is also studying full time, and being a parent to her child. Without the help of §43 support, Ditte is forced to take maximum loans, incurring escalating debts which will burden her for years to come. Determination and resilience are clearly present, yet she must navigate a perilous path. How many years must Ditte and her daughter survive under this stress before they become an economically viable family unit and what damage occurs along the way?

The political and psychological economy of lone motherhood

For many lone mothers such as Jette, Ditte and Mona, a strong investment in post-secondary education would be sound social policy. It is difficult to find consistent arguments for the refusals received by Ditte and Jette. Extra costs to the public for the social assistance educational benefit (§43) as opposed to the general state education grant (SU) and loans are small (see Appendix B). Seen from a broader perspective, public expenditures for Ditte and Jette would probably be much greater if they remained on full social assistance or received partial subsidies as a supplement to low, part-time wages. All available research data and a cost-benefit analysis support this argument: lone mothers who most frequently stay on social assistance for long periods are those mothers with minimal or no educational background (Ingerslev et al, 1992; Välfärdsprojektet, 1996).

In reality, for many years Denmark has had a strong social policy tradition supporting the education of lone mothers as a social investment promoting economically independent families. The former public organization Mødrehjælpen (Mothers' Help) and the new private Mothers' Help Organization established in 1983[1] have continuously included educational support for lone mothers at the centre of their agenda. Further, the 1976 Social Assistance Law clearly stated that social assistance for educational support should be given in cases where there was a threat of, or direct loss of, the capability to maintain a sufficient income. This social policy was one of several strategies to facilitate educational support for lone mothers.

However, the general economic crisis, combined with lack of professional knowledge within the municipalities about this area of social work practice, led to a severe reduction in the number of grants and to a reduction in educational support for lone mothers. In 1984, the Ministry of Social Affairs, after pressure from the new Mothers' Help Organization, released a circular to the municipalities stressing the importance of educational support to lone mothers through the Social Assistance Law, but this official reminder seems to have lost its influence on decisions made about educational support at many municipal social centres.

In the earlier drafts of the new Act on Active Social Policy, which was passed by the Danish Parliament (*Folketinget*) in 1997, and made effective on 1 July 1998, lone mothers were mentioned as one group for whom rehabilitative educational support could be given in cases of limited working capacity caused by physical, psychological, or social obstacles. However, neither in the final version of the law, nor in the directives to the law, was particular attention paid to lone mothers as a special category. They are covered like other groups under the general provisions of the law, which stresses work and activation programmes over and above any educational training (Socialministeriet, 1998). Although the new law, like the former law, emphasizes the importance of not depending on strict social or medical diagnostic categories when evaluating a person's need for rehabilitation, the mothers in our study have not received the educational support they are entitled to without a struggle, if at all.

Vulnerable lone mothers often do not have an easily identified social problem or tangible handicap, and as we have seen in the case narratives presented here, their vulnerabilities and problems are multiple and complex – often system-induced – so that many of their life situations cannot be contained within simple diagnostic categories (Egelund and Halskov, 1990). However, in all situations, material poverty and the constant struggle to make ends meet severely handicap educational aspirations, exacerbate psychological stress, place many strains on the parent–child relationship, and act as deterrents to educational success. It is only through the dogged persistence of women like Mona, Ditte and Jette that educational goals are kept alive. How many others give up their dreams because they cannot cope with the multiple obstacles in their paths?

Part I has presented detailed case portraits of six Danish lone mothers whose lives are variously scarred by the constant and chronic anxiety about economic instability, low-wage jobs, family violence, poor housing, sick children and restricted access to education. Together they share the same marginal status in society, often excluded from fundamental requirements for a decent standard of living. What happens, however, when that marginality is also embedded in another form of exclusion – the dual 'other' status of immigrant outsider and lone mother? In Part II the stories of ethnic minority lone mothers are told.

Note

[1] *Mødrehjælpen* (Mothers' Help Organization). From its start in 1923 the Mothers' Help Organization was privately financed, but in 1939 it received state financing in accordance with a new law providing support to mothers. This law stipulated that the Mothers' Help Organization should serve all mothers, both married, unmarried and pregnant. Mothers' Help Institutions were established all over Denmark.

This state-financed Mothers' Help Organization was abolished again in 1976, when the Act on Social Assistance (*Lov om Social Bistand*) was adopted. According to the Act, social support to all citizens was decentralized to the Municipal Social Administrations (*Socialforvaltningen*), and institutions for special groups, like the Mothers' Help Organization, were therefore regarded as unnecessary.

In the years after 1976 it became more and more evident that the special professional expertise and service that Mothers' Help Organizations (*Mødrehjælpen*) had possessed, had not been effectively transferred to the Municipal Social Administrations. Lone mothers, who had always been a vulnerable group in society, did not get sufficient support, and several surveys demonstrated that lone mothers experienced considerably worse living conditions than most other groups in society.

Consequently a group of private individuals decided to establish a new private organization, the Mothers' Help Organization of 1983 (*Mødrehjælpen af 1983*). The initiative received much attention from the public and media, and many local support groups were established all over Denmark.

One of the issues that the new Mothers' Help Organization of 1983 targeted was the decline in educational support for lone mothers, and the organization put great pressure on the Ministry of Social Affairs to emphasize the importance of educational support to lone mothers.

Part II:
The outsiders – the worlds of ethnic minority lone mothers

Ethnic minority lone mothers in Denmark

The isolation and lack of social support networks that low-income Danish lone mothers experience are exacerbated for immigrant lone mothers as they struggle to cope with the multiple stresses of lone motherhood in a foreign culture where they are ethnic minorities and frequent targets of discrimination. In the following chapter a detailed case study of Maria, an immigrant lone mother from Latin America, is presented, followed by briefer portraits of five additional lone mothers in order to explore the 'outsider' status that they occupy in Danish society. As with Maria, two of the lone mothers are from Latin America, one is from the Middle East, one from the Caribbean, and one from Greenland. The key themes that emerge in these women's lives are not unique, neither are they always specific to immigrant women; rather, many of the obstacles encountered are part of the fabric of most low-income lone mothers' lives in Denmark. However, as an ethnic minority lone mother, all these problems may increase exponentially – social isolation, weak networks, outsider status, stigmatization, discrimination on the streets, in housing agencies, and at the workplace. But the most damaging forms of discrimination occur when immigrant women are married to Danish men and become victims of domestic violence, for their rights as mothers are threatened as their foreign status frequently disadvantages them in terms of protection, custody and visitation arrangements. On the other hand, 'positive discrimination' in terms of obtaining access to an education through §43 emerges as a distinctive advantage for three of the six immigrant women; for being an 'outsider' may be viewed by the social welfare authorities as enough of a disadvantage in Danish society to make a case for investing in their education. In contrast to the Danish lone mothers interviewed, several ethnic minority lone mothers describe positive experiences at the social centres, and feel that they received "good help".

FIVE

Life on the margins

Maria and Diego

> "But I was all by myself and I was so unhappy.… I felt so alone and deserted."

Twenty-six-year-old Maria, an immigrant from Latin America, has experienced a series of crises since she became pregnant with her son, Diego, who is now three years old. Maria and her husband, both from Latin America, emigrated to Denmark, and shortly afterwards Maria moved with her husband to Southern Europe, where he worked as a musician. When Maria became pregnant, her husband abandoned her and she returned to Denmark late in her pregnancy only to find that she had lost her residency status; after several legal appeals were made on her behalf, she regained her residency status. While Maria initially stayed with her brother who also lives in Denmark, he was going through a difficult divorce and she could not remain there. Soon after her return to Denmark, Maria was hospitalized with a nervous breakdown and premature labour, and she remained in the hospital for over seven weeks as she had no place to live. A hospital social worker put her in contact with Egmontgården, where she was immediately offered a flat, and she moved there shortly before the birth of Diego.

Being alone and the struggle to cope in a foreign country

> "It was a very bad pregnancy and I cried very much every day … when I was in hospital I was very upset and I cried and cried so Diego has experienced a lot inside my stomach.… The birth itself went very well, five hours – but I was all by myself and I was so unhappy – I felt so alone and deserted."

Maria was referred to a psychologist by the health visitor at Egmontgården, and began seeing the psychologist on a regular basis. The environment at Egmontgården was supportive, but Maria finds it very difficult to cope with being alone and without family in a foreign country:

> "I could manage with money, and I had lots of support for my situation, but I don't have any family around me. And even if you have 700 Dkr to go and buy food, if you don't have the energy to get up and go, and no one to talk to and to help with the emotional things ... it's very hard when you're sick – at home I had my mother and sisters ... but taking care of a baby alone and no one to help when you're sick is a very hard thing."

While Maria struggles to cope with constant depression, she finds it difficult living in a building with so many lone mothers who have problems. However, she also establishes friendships with several other women at Egmontgården, including some Spanish-speaking lone mothers, and feels that, despite the problems, the setting has been a very "secure" place for her. As Maria reflects on her situation and compares Denmark to her native country, she observes:

> "Lone mothers in Denmark have a high status. They're protected ... when I compare to my sister at home where lone mothers are not protected and their status is very low ... there is no welfare, no nothing there.... Here there are a lot of hard things about being a lone mother but I try to look at it positively and I have gotten a lot of help."

However, as Maria prepares to leave Egmontgården and to search for a flat, her housing experience is fraught with discrimination:

> "I have to fight for myself, because I am living in a foreign country, and I speak another language, and I have to fight with the social housing agency.... I went there and both times I got a very bad housing counsellor who was racist – she did not treat me or Nina [another Black immigrant lone mother] well ... we had the same experience and she kind of looks down on us. She said, 'If you come with all these demands you have, it will take years before you have a flat' ... but the demands were my rights because before I had been living in Copenhagen seven years without one place to live. And I

said I am entitled to an apartment with three rooms, and then she got angry and said, 'You can't expect anything when you have demands like that'. A lot of the people who work there they're tired of all the people who make demands, but it's the foreigners who get the worst of it ... they take their frustrations out on the immigrants."

Maria also describes other situations where she has been a victim of racism:

"When it happens, when people are racist, I cannot go out. I stay home and I am afraid of going out and what will happen ... and I'm afraid of being nice to people and smiling at people because I don't know what they will give back to me.... Once there was a man who pushed me on a bus ... and I just stayed home from school for a week and I didn't want to go out ... and there have been people like old ladies pushing me on the street and shouting, 'Go back to your own country' and things like that.... It's very hard to understand when you yourself don't look down at other people why they should look down at you because of the colour of your skin, so I get a shock every time it happens."

Maria's educational opportunities and access to §43

While Maria has encountered racism in the housing agency, and on the streets of Copenhagen, she also believes that she has benefited from her foreigner status and that in terms of §43, she actually received preferential treatment because she was an immigrant lone mother – she applied for rehabilitation educational assistance (*revalidering*) to study as a social pedagogue:

"I very much tried to explain how much I wanted this education and that I plan to go on being a lone mother, and so I need this education to get a good job and earn money ... I think because I was unemployed for a long time they want to invest something in me so I could get an education and a job later because there is a great need for social pedagogues ... and because I was a foreigner they thought it was a good idea ... so it was not difficult for me to get it – but I know it has been difficult for others [Danish lone mothers], they know the system and have been applying to get §43 but they didn't get it ... and the social worker at Egmontgården helped and talked about my situation and the social worker at the social board heard about my situation and was nice ... so now in Denmark I know I will have a chance to have a career, now I have been given *revalidering* so I can look forward to having an education and working with children ... that is so exciting and I am happy about that."

Because Maria receives §43 rehabilitation assistance she is able to manage financially as she pays only 1,000 Dkr a month for her flat during her two-year stay at Egmontgården.

The educational practicum

Maria's first three-month practicum at an institution for people with mental disabilities involved inconvenient hours, where she had to work until 4.00 pm, and this was difficult for Diego, as she could no longer pick him up at 3.00 pm so he had to spend longer days at the day care:

"I was very tired and exhausted when I came home and I didn't have time or energy to be with Diego the same way as before ... the practicum time was so tough, and they wouldn't let me leave early in the day – they wanted to let me take one day off and work late the other days and I would rather have early days. I felt really bad because for two years I have been spending so much time with Diego and now I am away so much of the time and I have to study and it's so different from before. And I am not like I was with him before and his reaction is a problem."

Diego reacts very strongly to Maria's absence and stress and begins to regress, soiling his pants and having constant diarrhoea. This also follows several other changes – a move from Egmontgården and a new day care centre which all coalesce during this same time, creating multiple adjustments in Diego's life.

The move from Egmontgården to a new flat: coping with multiple changes

Maria describes the stressful move from Egmontgården in late summer and how she now struggles to cope alone in her new life as a student lone mother, saying, "Egmontgården was not just a help physically and socially, but the social workers and nurses are very good at giving you emotional support as well as psychological support to see things through".

As she had received moving expenses two years before when she and Diego moved to Egmontgården, she could not get any help from the social centre for this move, and this time she needed 12,000 Dkr for the flat deposit as well as furniture costs:

> "It was just a terrible time when we moved ... it was terrible – just a week before I had to do my practicum for my studies – and all of this was in July ... I thought I would go crazy ... and I didn't have anyone to help with the move except for two friends from Egmontgården ... and Diego was not in day care and I had to apply for a loan and all kinds of paper stuff had to be done and I had to take Diego to all the offices because he was on holiday from day care, and I was also training him not to use diapers – it was very stressful. Diego could not take his nap as I had to take him to the offices and they close at 2 o' clock and it was hot and he was reacting ... and I had to pack everything every night until 12 or 1 o'clock and I never had a chance to rest.... It was very exhausting."

In addition to the stress of moving, Maria also broke up with her boyfriend who she had been seeing for over four months just before she moved, and the break-up was difficult for Diego who had become attached to the boyfriend.

Maria and Diego: social networks and social isolation

Since leaving Egmontgården, it has become much harder for Maria to manage. She likes the new flat which is very spacious, but the neighbourhood has many alcoholics and she does not want Diego to grow up there. Despite the fact that Maria has friends and some limited contact with her brother, she still feels very alone and isolated:

> "I have friends and a lot of people I know but since I've had Diego I've been disappointed. They kind of let me down – because if something happens, my friends have their own lives and their own responsibilities – but I need someone as a lone mother who I can rely on ... and of course I have friends who help with Diego if I

know ahead of time, but even then it's hard to find someone who can help – but it is really a problem when there is an unexpected situation like in my practicum I was so exhausted.... I started fainting and Diego was alone and I called friends and they couldn't come to help and I was crying so much ... because I felt so alone and no one could come and help me – twice it happened and one time my brother came and he could see I was really ill and he called the doctor and the doctor gave me some strong drugs ... and another time I had the 'flu and a high fever and I called my best friend, but she didn't come because she was going to a party ... and twice I've been so bad off that I felt suicidal and I haven't talked to anyone about this."

After Maria survives the stress of her first practicum, with both physical and emotional costs for herself and Diego, she begins to search for some child care help during times of high stress and sickness, and finds that there is a "grandmother project" which would supply her with a 'grandmother' to babysit for 20 Dkr an hour during the day, and 30 Dkr an hour at night. This presents Maria with the need for additional financial assistance, so Maria requests a babysitting subsidy from the social centre. During this period, Maria's health is bad – she suffers from debilitating migraines, back problems, and a hernia, and expresses continuing concern about the impact of her stressful existence and her depression on Diego:

"During Easter I was very depressed, and it has been really really hard. I feel it is so difficult to have Diego home for such a long time [over the holidays] and when I'm tired I often take it out on him and I'll admit I am sometimes very hard on him."

As Maria continues to study in the social pedagogue programme, she insightfully and painfully analyses her own conflicting emotions towards her son, as well as her mothering practices, stating:

"I have always invested a lot of time on myself and Diego and I want to be a good mother and do all the right things for him, but sometimes I have been so tired and stressed and I became authoritarian and of course he reacted because he was not used to me being like that.... The more knowledge I get about children, the more upset I get with myself when I think about Diego, and then I have a bad conscience ... the first two years I really tried to control my temper towards

Diego, which meant that he was a very balanced and healthy boy. But now it has changed – what I give to him, I get back – when I'm aggressive I get it back ... he has changed incredibly much ... physically and intellectually he is doing well, he is a bright boy, but psychologically it's not so good ... I know how to change the bad pattern between Diego and me but I'm just too tired.... I have often been sick sometimes quite badly. Diego has experienced some bad things when I have thrown up again and again and then he would get mad at me. Sometimes I've wished for someone to come and take that child away from me – that's the way I have felt sometimes."

Maria's sense of feeling overwhelmed leads her to talk with her social worker to find out if Diego could get a 'weekend family', but unfortunately there is a long waiting list. Maria feels that "a family who could have him sometimes, would be a good solution", and clearly would relieve some of the pressure she feels about her son. Maria describes Diego as physically well developed and very verbal, fluent in both Danish and Spanish:

"He is only three years old but he can have conversations in both languages – he is bright, very bright, good at games, and nice. He is a fast learner. He likes to 'read' books and knows the books by heart – he has always been very advanced for his age in both his motor development and his language ... but I think he has a hard time figuring out where he is emotionally. It is a problem that he relates so aggressively toward other people ... when he meets other people he feels threatened maybe because he is afraid of losing me.... He gets very annoyed and aggressive towards other people if they want to talk to me but if it's people he knows, it's okay. When we meet other children when we are out, his first reaction is to become very aggressive – the other day he just went over to a strange man and hit him with a stick, and I got very, very upset with him."

Maria feels that her relationship with Diego is so intense because she is a lone mother, and that he is too dependent on her and feels very concerned about her, often unhealthily so:

"I have a lot of fights with Diego, because he is so closely connected to me, and I think it's too bad for him that he has to live so intensely with me, he is very concerned with me, whether I am happy or sad and he asks me all the time, 'Mom are you happy, are you sad, are you sick, are you tired?' I think it's too bad for him that he should be concerned with me being sad or if I get upset. It has never been so hard for me to control my temper."

Just before Diego's third birthday, a home visit is made to Maria's new flat:

Diego appears hyperactive and very demanding of his mother's attention. He doesn't concentrate on any activity for a long period of time, and when Maria talks with me [the observer] he reacts angrily, kicks the floor, hits his mother and screams, throws the toys around the room and begins to pull out the electric plugs. Maria runs after him and reprimands him calmly, although she soon becomes angry. When I begin to play with Diego again, he stops and says he would like to visit me. When I prepare to leave he becomes aggressive, and does not want me to leave, crawling over me. Maria appears to be uncomfortable and remarks that he is like that around other adults who demand her attention. It is clear that Diego is a bright verbal child who expresses frustration and anger, and demands constant attention from his mother. Their relationship during this visit is marked by tension and conflict.

Diego's day care experience

Diego attended an infant day care centre from about 10 months of age, until he was two years old, and when Maria moved from Egmontgården she enrolled him in a new centre in August 1996. Initially Maria felt that the pedagogues were very supportive of both her and Diego, and described Diego as "very happy there". During Maria's first practicum, when she was ill and largely unavailable for him, he developed a stomach problem and would soil his pants just before she picked him up. She describes this as a very frustrating and worrisome period and felt very supported by the pedagogues at the day care centre, who initially urged her to take him to the doctor as he seemed to have diarrhoea. Maria did see the doctor, but fortunately the test results were normal. They concluded that Diego was reacting to her stress, the multiple changes, and her lack of time with him:

"It's almost everyday like a reaction ... or a kind of revenge. But he never does it at home. Only when I have to do homework and then he gets upset and can do it. But they are very nice at the kindergarten – the pedagogues tried to help change the pattern so that he is clean when I come ... and if I come and he is dirty they change him instead of me – for four months he messed in his pants ... and I was so tired of it and washing so many clothes all the time and I got upset. But after the pedagogue and I decided that she should change and wash him when it happened, it stopped after a while. Now it has stopped – he is clean and can control his toilet visits."

Although Diego likes the day care and seems to be doing well there, after about six months Maria becomes very critical of the staff and the centre, feeling that they are no longer supportive of her and Diego:

"In the beginning they treated me well but since I started saying things about how they treat the parents and children, they got annoyed. I think they are threatened by me because I am doing a practicum in another day care centre which has a very different structure. [Diego's] day care is a strain and they are not listening to how he is doing."

After Maria's dissatisfaction with the day care centre she arranges to move him and he begins at another new centre in August 1997. At 3.4 months he is observed at the new centre after he has attended for two months:

Diego is sitting on the lap of the male pedagogue, crawling on him and talking to him, and talking about the other children on the swings which Diego has just left after a conflict with two boys. The pedagogue plays warmly with him and Diego laughs as the pedagogue bobs him up and down on his shoulders. Diego continues to crawl on him and hug him, then he runs over to the other boys and he stands looking at them as they swing. He plays with a stick in the sand and joins another child on the swings. Soon a conflict ensues as the boy tries to turn Diego around on the swing. Diego screams, "Stop it, stop it" and the boy tells Diego to get off the swing. Diego refuses and another child tells Diego "He had the swing first". Diego is crying, saying, "I came, I came" [trying to say he was also playing there] and the other boy kicks him. Diego says, "I go home this minute, I go now"; as the other boy calls him "stupid", Diego shouts,

"I'm not stupid". Diego walks off again, kicks some toys on the ground, finds a bike and sits on it, still alone. He walks away to find a pedagogue, with slow and resigned movements. The pedagogue helps him with a bike and he rides around by himself. Soon the children are called in for fruit, and Diego is quiet; he goes to play in the nap room as the pedagogue asks him to sit down. He continues to look at a book and shows some of the pictures to other children. Diego again goes into the nap room, and is asked to sit down again by a pedagogue. He finds a book about a circus which he is excited about and the pedagogue suggests they read it while fruit is served. Diego agrees and hands over the book. As cups are handed out Diego tries to grab the others but is told to sit down and wait his turn, which he does. He is very calm and focused during the circus story, and interacts well with the other children. As they are shown circus pictures he asks, curiously, "Why do they sleep there?".

Although Diego experienced conflicts with some of the boys outside, his coping strategy appeared to be to cry and walk away. However, he also seemed to recover quickly from such conflicts and interacted well with children in the quiet and more structured setting of snack and story. He sought out the pedagogues when he needed help, but was not overly dependent on them. During an interview with Diego's pedagogue (with his mother present), the pedagogue perceived Diego as having adjusted well to the day care with no more than "normal problems", stating, "He is doing very well. If he does something wrong you can talk to him and he listens to you and does what he is told". She describes Diego as a child who shows a lot of initiative and that he concentrates particularly well when an adult is present. While the pedagogue states that Diego "screams and shouts and can be very demanding if he doesn't get what he wants", she also comments positively on his social interactions with other children, and his "positive way of contacting other adults. If he has problems he asks for help, but doesn't hang around the adults a lot".

During the interview Maria also tells the pedagogue how she regrets losing her temper with Diego, and refers to an incident where she became so angry that she told him she would leave him and she went out on the stairs. After Diego became fearful and called for her, Maria went back inside, regretting her actions, and told the pedagogue, "I should never do anything like that". During the recounting of this episode, the pedagogue listened supportively and in a non-judgmental way told Maria that it was good she was aware of that, and that it was an important first step along the way, saying, "We all do things to our children that we later regret". Maria also expressed her continuing concern that Diego feels responsible for her, and behaves in a pseudo-adult like manner. She describes how, recently, she lay on the bed, crying, and Diego came to comfort her, caressing her cheek and saying, "easy, easy". The atmosphere during the interview was supportive, and Maria openly talked to the pedagogue about the problems and concerns she has about Diego. From the centre observation and the pedagogue's comments, Diego appears to be adjusting well to the new centre and in marked contrast to the home visit, four months earlier, there are signs that he is learning to cope with his frustrations, and that he is developing good relationships with the adults and children.

A vulnerable and determined lone mother in a foreign culture

Maria has experienced a multitude of stressful events that began prior to Diego's birth. Abandoned when pregnant by her husband in a foreign country, her self-esteem very low, and with nowhere to turn, she returned to Denmark for help, and Maria has since determinedly pursued whatever help was available. Despite the discrimination she experienced at the housing agency and from Danish people on the streets, she has also received preferential treatment because of her immigrant status, and was approved for support under §43 to pursue a career as a social pedagogue. Coping with the stresses of being a socially isolated lone mother, far away from her native country, with severe health problems and critical self-doubts about her ability as a mother, she is torn by conflicting emotions about her young son. He, too, has been severely affected by his mother's emotional instability, and has reacted with anger and fear to the unpredictable changes and emotional turmoil he has experienced, with behaviour that has ranged from aggression and regression to protectiveness. The day care centre that Diego now attends has been a vital support service for both Maria and Diego, providing Diego with a supportive developmentally appropriate setting to which he has adjusted well, and where he has formed a child social network. The pedagogues have also been supportive of Maria and understanding of her stressful existence. Maria has a flimsy support network, which unravelled after she left Egmontgården. The time demands of an intense educational programme and caring for a young child, plus the ongoing social isolation, frequently threaten to overwhelm Maria and stretch her beyond her coping abilities. However, Maria is determined to use whatever support services she can obtain, and more recently she has managed to find a 'weekend family' for Diego and the social centre has approved her request for additional babysitting subsidies, both of which will ease the burdens of Maria's lone mother existence. Maria, educated and aware of her rights as a lone mother and immigrant, has been able to successfully access the public welfare system which has provided her with supportive services and enabled her to pursue a path out of poverty.

Carmina and her three children

Carmina is a 30-year-old Latin American mother of three young children, two toddler boys and a four-year-old girl. Carmina is living at a crisis centre, having fled from her abusive Danish husband to whom she has been married for six years. Carmina was trained as a health care assistant in her native country, and worked for a brief period in Denmark. After the birth of her children, she was licensed as a family day care provider and took care of her own and other children in her home. The family lived in a rural area of Denmark and her husband, who worked for the government, spent long periods of time away from home. He became abusive and violent after the birth of the children and this continued for several years until he threw Carmina and the children out of the house; she then sought help at a crisis centre in Copenhagen.

Living with violence: abused by her husband and his family

Carmina relates abusive and racist encounters with her parents-in-law after she and her husband returned to Denmark following their marriage in her native country. She describes how her alcoholic mother-in-law hit her when she visited, and her father-in-law offered to pay her to leave Denmark:

> "He said to me, I'll give you 20,000 Dkr to go back to [her country], he wanted to buy me ... he told me they wanted my husband to marry a Danish girl, no black foreign girl from another country ... and whenever I go to their house they make me pay 3 Dkr for a cup of coffee ... in my country I never heard of that ... there are many

people with no money but they never would say you must pay to drink a cup of coffee in their house ... it was terrible for me ... they were no good and I had just come to Denmark."

The marriage does not turn out well for Carmina. She is left alone for long periods of time when her husband travels, and feels extremely isolated. After the birth of the children, her husband turns violent, demands sex from her as soon as he returns from a trip, and if she does not comply, he beats her. As the beatings continue, the children also become victims:

"He said I had only time for the children and he was jealous ... he said if he comes home Saturday, I have to have sex with him and give attention to him, not the children ... but I said, 'I cannot, now we have three children and they have to eat, shower, I have to wash clothes and take care of them', but he did not care about them or me – he would beat me in front of the children, and they screamed and cried shouting, 'No, no, don't hit mother', but he didn't care."

As the situation worsened her husband sold the house without her knowledge and told Carmina and the children to leave. She says, "He threw us into the street and I cried and said to him, 'Please no, because of the children'". Isolated, with no network to turn to, and ignorant of her legal rights, Carmina is desperate and rents a room from her mother-in-law's alcoholic boyfriend, who then sexually molests her. She flees with the children and contacts a crisis centre in Copenhagen. At that point, the social centre in Copenhagen will not help her, as they say it is the responsibility of her former social centre to pay moving expenses and to give her social assistance. Not only does Carmina face housing and financial problems, but she has also lost everything from her former life: "He took the house, my furniture, he stole my things, he took the money and I don't know the law in Denmark". Her husband has also listed the children as living at his new address in Copenhagen and is receiving both the child and family allowances. Carmina complained to the social centre and they agreed it was a violation of the law, but have done nothing about it.

Violence, discrimination, and custody of the children

Carmina's biggest battle now revolves around custody of the children who are living with her at the crisis centre, but they see their father at his new flat in Copenhagen every week. Carmina says that the children are afraid of their father who beats them and is very harsh. Carmina has been assisted at the crisis centre by a counsellor, who has contacted a lawyer on her behalf, and the custody issue is now before the court. Carmina, who does not speak fluent Danish, feels that her foreigner status puts her at a disadvantage, particularly as her husband is well educated and has a good government job. She relates how her husband has lied about their situation:

> "I'm not sure they will believe me ... he says he took care of the children for these years and he says I take bad care of them, and that's not true and everyone at our home where I lived before knows that ... and my husband tells so many lies ... and the children are afraid of him ... he beats them and they cry ... and he doesn't want the children but he wants to hurt me and that's why he wants to take the children away from me ... and I am so afraid, because they are my life ... he can keep the money but the children I cannot give up – I cannot lose my children."

Carmina's life as a foreigner in Denmark has been fraught with multiple forms of violence and discrimination. Since her arrival, she has been rejected by her husband's family and has been unable to form a social network due to her isolated living situation, and her status as a foreigner. Since the birth of her children she has been a victim of her husband's violence, and she and the children endured a frightening domestic existence until she fled to the crisis centre. Having lost her home and her possessions, she turns to the social authorities for help, but finds that she is caught between two social centres who initially refuse to take responsibility for her situation. Her terror of losing custody of her children consumes her, and she now awaits the court's custody decision. The family violence, her terror of losing her children, and the instability of living at the crisis centre have severely affected the children, who she describes as clinging to her and fearful of the enforced weekly visits to their father. Although both Carmina and the children have been the victims of the father's violence, that does not appear to be a significant factor in the determination of custody.

Carmina's current and future realities

Carmina would like to return home to her native country, but cannot leave Denmark with the children. She is struggling to cope with life at the crisis centre and to support her children, who are so fearful that they do not want to leave her in the mornings to attend day care. Her own psychological health is fragile – she has nightmares about the traumatic assaults and about losing her children. Her situation is desperate and she fears that discrimination will again be reflected in the custody decision, saying, "If my husband gets the children my life is finished. I cannot live! Without my children I cannot live".

Carmina's future as an isolated immigrant mother in Denmark is tenuous. Even if she does succeed in retaining custody of the children, she still faces severe housing problems finding a suitable flat for herself and her three young children. She and the children have suffered greatly from the turmoil and family violence, and the psychological health of the children will be impaired if they continue to be the victims of their father's violence. Carmina's vulnerability as a battered wife with no social network further exacerbates her family's vulnerability, and her status as an immigrant lone mother may adversely affect her entry into the labour market. In short, Carmina's situation reveals disturbing violations of her rights as a woman, as a mother, and as a foreigner.

Adriana, Carl and Anna

Adriana is the 30-year-old mother of 10-year-old Carl and two-year-old Anna. Adriana grew up in an impoverished family in a small village in her native Latin America, and did not have many educational opportunities during her childhood and adolescence. Ten years ago Adriana came to Denmark with her Danish boyfriend, and soon afterwards they were married. She became pregnant with their son, and shortly after his birth, her husband became violent. She left him after the second assault, and she and her son led an unstable existence, moving from place to place as she searched for suitable housing. After she met Anna's father and became pregnant by him, she applied for a flat at Egmontgården and has been living there for two years with her daughter. Her son has been living with his father since he was three years old.

Violence and loss of custody

Adriana's husband became angry and violent soon after the birth of Carl, and Adriana describes that period as "a very sad time ... with so many problems and he never understood me ... he got angry so fast". Carl's father assaulted Adriana twice, resulting in two hospital visits. The first time he hit her in the stomach, and Adriana called the police, but they did not believe her, as he told them she had provoked him, and as she says, "I could not speak good Danish and he lied to the police so nothing happened". The second time, when he punched her in the face, she decided to leave with Carl who was then two years old. Carl's father and Adriana were divorced with joint custody but that disadvantaged Adriana as she was afraid of her ex-husband and he made all the decisions: "He decided about Carl alone and I had no choice ... so there were a lot of problems as I never had any chance to decide about my son ... because in his eyes [Carl's father] I am nothing". Carl's father had placed Carl on the waiting list for day care in his municipality, and when he received a place, he demanded custody of Carl, who was then three years old. Adriana protested, they went back to court, but as the court had awarded joint custody, they said it was up to the parents to work out living arrangements. Adriana was very upset, but felt powerless to challenge the Danish courts and was afraid of her ex-husband's anger and threats, so she relinquished custody and has continued to see her son every second weekend.

Educational and economic realities

While Adriana suffered abusive treatment from her ex-husband and was very distressed about the custody decision seven years ago, she has now built a new life for herself with her young daughter, and is appreciative of the support she has received at Egmontgården and from the social worker there. Because she has back problems and she is a foreign lone mother, her social worker encouraged her to apply for §43 and she was recently notified that she has been approved, and her young daughter is now attending day care. Adriana is excited about the opportunity to pursue an education, and after she completes high school, she plans to pursue training in dress design.

"They really give you good help here in Denmark ... at home in my country they do nothing for lone mothers, either the family must help you or nothing ... now I'm happy to live in Denmark and I'm happy for my children ... I have learned to be independent and to live alone ... Denmark is like school for me, I have learned so many things here."

Adriana is currently searching for a flat as she has been at Egmontgården since Anna's birth two years ago, and hopes to find an affordable place as the rent at Egmontgården is very low which has made her economic situation viable: "Living here I have a good flat and it's been very easy to save money". She has been to the social housing agency and has listed her name with various housing organizations and is optimistic that she will find something, because so far she has received "good help".

Social networks and discrimination

Adriana has several Latin American friends and is on good terms with both Anna's father and Carl's Danish grandmother. She also describes herself as wanting to make friends with Danish women, but finds it difficult "as they talk to me nice but they think I am different". She recounts some prejudicial treatment from the health visitor who wondered "why my daughter is so white", and isolated incidents of ethnic insults on the street, which she says do not bother her that much. Adriana regards the Danish Prince's marriage to a "non-white girl who is a foreigner" as a very positive step, believing "that will keep racism quiet". However, in general she focuses on the positive support she has received at Egmontgården and from her social centre, saying, "Being an immigrant here in Denmark is OK ... it doesn't matter if you're Danish or not, they will help you".

Adriana and the future

Adriana reports that her son is doing well in school and that he has a good relationship with his father and with her. He is very attached to his little sister and likes to take care of her when he visits. Adriana is optimistic about her future and looks forward to beginning her education in the coming year: "Now I say to myself, I can go to school,

I will get a good education and when I am 34 I will be finished and I like to work here in Denmark ... I want to become somebody". Although Adriana's early experiences in Denmark were traumatic, she is resilient and appears to have recovered from those early struggles and expresses high expectations for her future. In contrast to the poverty she left behind in her native country, Adriana appreciates the social safety net in Denmark, and the fact that she has been able to lead a viable existence as a lone mother with the opportunity for an education, saying, "Here in Denmark they help you, and if you are a lone mother, they help you more".

Emilie, Maja and Pania

Thirty-four-year-old Emilie, an immigrant from Greenland, lives alone in a modern flat in a town north of Copenhagen with her two daughters, six-year-old Maja and two-year-old Pania. They moved to Denmark a year ago when Rasmus, Emilie's husband and Pania's father, accepted a one-year post-graduate study position paid for by his employer in Greenland. The family decided they would all move together because they felt it would be too hard emotionally to be separated from each other for such a long time. Emilie, after working as a clerical assistant for five years, quit her job because she could not get leave, and the family gave up their apartment in Greenland. Soon after their move to Denmark, Rasmus began drinking heavily and began beating Emilie. Emilie decided to flee with her daughters, and now, as a lone mother, she faces an impending divorce, an upcoming court case for custody of Pania, and she and her daughters are still suffering from the effects of domestic violence. While Emilie has survived so far with the help of a private crisis centre, her needs have not been met by the social system, and her future in Denmark with both her daughters is uncertain.

Fleeing domestic violence

Emilie says that even though she knew Rasmus was drinking heavily every day, their first months together after moving to Denmark seemed to be going well. She sometimes felt threatened by Rasmus when he was drunk, but "Rasmus had only beaten me a little and only a few times when he was drunk". Then, one night several months ago, after sharing a cosy dinner with friends in their own apartment, Rasmus, who was very drunk, suddenly became extremely angry and grabbed Emilie and attempted to strangle her. Rasmus had never done that before, and a shocked Emilie ran into the bedroom where her daughters were sleeping. Some hours later, while her children watched him, Rasmus started to assault Emilie again. She was afraid to stay the rest of the night in their apartment with Rasmus, so she fled with Maja and Pania to stay with a friend. The friend helped her contact a crisis centre, and Emilie and the children moved there the next day. With hindsight, Emilie says she should have gone to a hospital or contacted the police, but when she first left Rasmus, she didn't want to involve the public system. She and her children stayed at the crisis centre for about two weeks before moving back into their apartment with Rasmus. Emilie says she felt pressured to return because Rasmus' parents came for a long visit with them. Also, she explains, the social centre told Emilie several times that it was very expensive for them to pay for her and the children to live at the crisis centre, and "when I was stupid enough to say that I could live with Rasmus, they would not pay any longer".

Emilie did not feel afraid of Rasmus as long as his parents were visiting, but as soon as they left, Rasmus started to abuse her again; screaming at her, shouting, and making wild accusations against her. Emilie decided she could not endure the abuse any longer and she and her daughters moved back to the crisis centre. By this time the traumatic effects of the abuse had caused Emilie severe physical symptoms: allergic eczema on her neck and daily nausea and vomiting. One month into their second stay at the crisis centre, Emilie was told by the social centre that she, Maja and Pania had to move again, and they would be relocated to one room in a hotel because this would be a cheaper way for the municipality to solve their housing problems. The hotel was very noisy, dirty and situated close to a busy road. Emilie felt completely lost. She could not believe that her own and her daughters' extremely difficult emotional situation was not taken into consideration when the social centre decided to move them into the hotel. "Only the money decided", says Emilie bitterly. The staff at the private crisis centre protested and continued to support Emilie by negotiating with the social centre; however, Emilie and her daughters were only permitted to move back there once the crisis centre agreed to pay the difference in cost between living in the hotel room and living in the crisis centre.

Emilie and her children: anxieties and a custody case

In the last few months, Maja and Pania have had regular contact with Rasmus, but the situation is very tense, and Emilie feels under constant pressure. Rasmus wants custody of his biological daughter, Pania, and he wants to take her back to Greenland. Emilie wants to stay in Denmark because she would like to get another job and an education, and the housing market in Greenland is bad. Emilie expresses misgivings about the impending court case for custody of Pania, and does not know whether Rasmus' violence will influence the custody decision in her favour. She also expresses anxieties about her attorney: "I do not know if I have confidence in her, but I have to believe she will do what she can for me".

As Emilie waits for the court case, she also has to cope with Pania's emotional upheaval – Pania has reacted to the last months' events by throwing tantrums and raging for hours against her. Her older daughter, Maja, whose biological father lives in Greenland, continually competes for her mother's attention and has had a conflictual relationship with Rasmus all through the marriage. Emilie comments, "They are both very stubborn and neither of them will compromise ... but Maja does not want to live with Rasmus again". Emilie, who cries continually as she talks in front of the children about the trauma of the violence, and the humiliation she has endured, is very open with them about the situation with Rasmus, and the children have both witnessed Rasmus' violent behaviour towards her.

Living alone in a foreign country

Emilie is alone and does not have many friends in Denmark, and her large extended family lives in Greenland. She has told her family about her difficult situation, and while they accept her decision to divorce Rasmus, none of them can help her directly in her present situation. Since she has left the crisis centre, Emilie has found a public housing flat in one of the municipal buildings. The flat is newly renovated and spacious, and Emilie furnishes it by restoring furniture from second-hand shops. She is very grateful for the practical and emotional assistance she has received from the crisis centre, and also for the help from one family counsellor at the social centre.

Although she has found a flat and made arrangements for Pania to begin day care and for Maja to begin school, Emilie and her daughters have been through a very stressful time and are still in unsettled circumstances. When they lived in Greenland, both of her children were in day care, but since moving to Denmark, Emilie has taken care of them herself, "24 hours around the clock". Emilie desperately wishes to establish a normal, stable, everyday life with her daughters. As Emilie reflects on her status as a Greenlander and as a survivor of domestic violence, she says,

> "I do not know what other people think of me coming from Greenland and being a victim of violence. I try not to think about it in that way. I do not think of myself primarily as a Greenlandian person but as a human being like everyone else. I do not want to be separated from people in that way. I consider myself a person on equal footing with others and do not think I have experienced prejudice toward myself or my situation."

It appears that Emilie's two most distressing experiences are now over: the trauma of violence and the total lack of understanding about her dangerous situation by the social centre. The advocacy and economic support from the private crisis centre became her salvation against the indifference of the public welfare system. However, the outcome of the custody case continues to create instability and high levels of anxiety for Emilie. It is unclear how much weight will be given to Rasmus' violent behaviour and, like so many other mothers who are victims of domestic violence, the court may not rule in her favour. Emilie's right to live in safety with her children is threatened, and she feels powerless to protect the rights of her younger child to a safe and secure childhood.

Zeinab and Yasser

> "But I think I am a mother now. Before I was not; I was too young and did not know what to do."

Twenty-six-year-old Zeinab is from the Middle East, and because of her father's political activities there, she was not allowed to attend school or university. Her parents decided to send her to Canada for further education, but during her exile, Zeinab became stranded in Turkey because her parents had been cheated on her flight tickets. While she was in Turkey, Zeinab married a Muslim man from her native country. She soon became pregnant, and Yasser was born in Turkey. After Yasser was born, Zeinab went to Denmark with Yasser's father who had lived in Denmark for many years. Zeinab was only 16 years old and Yasser a new-born when they arrived in Denmark. After staying with her husband in a provincial town in Denmark for four years, Zeinab decided to divorce him because he was violent and they had many conflicts:

> "I was hit a lot by Yasser's father, but Yasser only witnessed it once. He has only seen his father throw the dishes around the kitchen and things like that. Yasser has also been hit by his father, usually not so much, but once it was serious and I was also choked. I don't remember what happened, but he smashed Yasser against the wall."

Zeinab only went to the police once about her husband's violence but then withdrew her accusation as, "It does not help to put him in jail and then just send him out again". Soon after her divorce, she moved with Yasser to Copenhagen.

Zeinab's struggle to adjust to life alone in Denmark

While Zeinab and her ex-husband are Muslims, they are not fundamentalists, and Zeinab, who is well educated in her religious tradition, follows a spiritual path without any rigid adherence to religious customs and rituals. Since Zeinab moved to Copenhagen with Yasser, long periods have elapsed between her visits with her family back home in the Middle East, and she has experienced periods of loneliness and isolation which were particularly difficult when she had to cope with health problems. Even now Zeinab knows very few Danish people; most of her friends are immigrants and her boyfriend is from Africa. Zeinab feels that nobody really helped her during her difficult years as a very young lone mother, and that she had to cope all alone with her problems, which included a very insecure housing situation. Recently, however, her life has taken a turn for the better as she has received help from Boligfonden in finding a flat of her own, and she also feels positive about her current social worker at the social centre, after suffering many hurtful and discriminatory experiences with a former social worker in the provincial town that she lived with her husband: "She was a racist ... [who disliked Zeinab because] I came from a foreign country".

For most of her years as a lone mother, Zeinab and Yasser have lived on social assistance. This has been extremely difficult for Zeinab to manage because she was accustomed to a much higher standard of living before she became a lone mother. She has frequently called her father, who still lives in the Middle East, for help when her monthly social assistance amount has run out. Housing has also been a constant problem since Zeinab left her husband and moved to Copenhagen. She has had to move constantly, living with her brother for a period of time, and experienced a brief period of homelessness before receiving a small low-rent flat at the Boligfonden communal house for lone parents. But Zeinab experienced many cultural conflicts living with Danish lone parents, and felt stressed by the living situation. She was critical of Danish children's behaviour and the casual child-rearing approach of their parents which differed from her own, remarking, "They allowed their children to interrupt the grown-ups' conversations whenever the children wanted to". After she moved out of the Boligfonden house, she briefly shared a flat with another family, before moving to her boyfriend's very small flat. But a short time ago, Zeinab finally found a small flat of her own. Despite Zeinab's unstable housing conditions, she has struggled to maintain a home in the same neighbourhood. She did not want Yasser to change schools more than once.

During the previous year, Zeinab worked as a cleaning assistant at a large office for several months. She worked at night in order to earn more money, and had to leave Yasser alone while he slept. She would then come home in the morning and wake him for school and sleep while Yasser was at school. Zeinab enjoyed working and was proud of earning a salary for herself, but she had to give up that job because it was too exhausting for her and Yasser. During this time, Zeinab also had serious health problems which have now improved as her family life stabilized. Zeinab said that in the past she was almost constantly dizzy and fainted very often. She received help from a psychologist who worked with her "to try to solve [my] problems instead of going around fainting". Zeinab has received §43 educational support and attended several courses and completed the first part of her HF high school studies (see Chapter 3, Note 4); however, she has now taken a temporary break from school but hopes to continue receiving educational support when she resumes in the future.

Yasser's experiences

Yasser, now 10 years old, likes his school and is a successful student academically. He has many friends, although he is the only ethnic minority child in his class. He visits his father every other weekend and, according to Zeinab, the relationship is often difficult for him. Zeinab has never talked with Yasser about his father's violence, but she related that, "Yasser was like a flower folding itself out after his father moved out". Yasser recently told his mother that he understands why she loves her new boyfriend – because he does not hit her! Zeinab describes the conflictual pattern of interactions that ensues when Yasser visits his father:

> "His father tries to get back at me, and then Yasser gets confused. His father doesn't think I take care of him well enough.... He said that Yasser is not happy. Then I became very confused and asked Yasser if he would like to stay with his father. Yasser cried and said that he would like to stay with me."

Yasser's parents have strong disagreements about child-rearing. Zeinab is concerned that Yasser and his father watch violent and erotic adult movies together until late at night. Yasser's father also has trouble getting Yasser to do what he asks him to do, for example, taking a bath when told to do so. Yasser often becomes extremely angry and rages against his father. He never behaves that way with his mother who says that she is far stricter with him. Zeinab has custody, and despite the conflicts between herself and Yasser's father, she is willing to put up with a lot in order to help Yasser keep in touch with his father – she believes it is important for his development. Zeinab describes her own relationship with Yasser as very close and attached:

> "We are more like friends than like mother and son.... I had to tell him about the problems, for example, that we didn't have money for clothes. He could understand it and has never asked for sweets and extras. He has always been a little grown-up boy. He understands more than his age.... He is happy now, but he has been very much affected by all the changes. He would cry a lot if I didn't pick him up from school, and if I left him somewhere, he would also cry. I always explained to him that I would come back again, but he didn't understand it.... He is very attached to me. It is like I am God to him, and he does everything I tell him to do."

Zeinab and Yasser: facing the future

From a very young age, Zeinab has lived as a lone mother with her son, Yasser, in a foreign country, after leaving her violent husband and obtaining a divorce. Zeinab's own family lives far away and Zeinab has been isolated with her son in Danish society, and in a critical time of need, she received scarce support from the social system. Although she has now received §43 educational support, she has not managed to complete any formal Danish school training or education, as she has led a very unstable existence plagued by domestic violence, housing problems, cultural conflicts, discrimination and ill-health, while struggling to take care of her son. Zeinab has not been able to find consistent, culturally sensitive, and comprehensive social supports which clearly would go a long way towards easing her transition into Danish society and coping with her life as a vulnerable uneducated lone mother. While her son has adjusted well to Danish life, their future remains tenuous as Zeinab recently became pregnant and now awaits the birth of her second child.

Deborah and Sarah

Twenty-five-year-old Deborah is from the Caribbean, and she lives alone with her 18-month-old daughter, Sarah, who recently began attending day care. Deborah, who has a bachelor's degree from her native country, has been living in Denmark since her marriage three years ago. She is now separated from her Danish husband, and they have joint custody of Sarah, who lives with Deborah. Deborah has been struggling to find an affordable flat in Copenhagen and is currently receiving social assistance. As Deborah's four-year university degree is not recognized in Denmark, she has applied for §43 to continue her education, and she is now studying Danish so that she can gain admission to the university.

Deborah has experienced a very stressful two years as her marriage disintegrated soon after her daughter's birth, and when she decided to leave her husband "after a very rough time", which she describes as filled with "fighting and arguing and not being happy", she found herself stranded with no place to live. A private agency referred her to Egmontgården where she has been temporarily staying, while searching for a flat.

Alone and trapped as a foreigner: economic and social realities

Deborah expresses great frustration about her situation. She has clear educational aspirations and wants to develop a career as an English teacher or translator so that she will be economically independent. She is returning to school to take Danish classes with the hope of being admitted to the university. However, she is struggling to cope with financial problems, no suitable housing, and the conflicting demands of studying, and being a mother, in a foreign country:

> "It's hard ... I don't know if I can do it ... I study and take care of my child and I'll probably have to have a job as well ... and I don't know ... it's three things in one – three major things and it's too difficult ... and I'm a foreigner ... and I'm trying to see if I can get some support [§43] from my social centre, but it's difficult to get help from them. You really have to be an alcoholic or drug user or really some psychopath to get some help. I mean I really need some help to help me to get back into society ... but they don't think I have too many social problems – but being a lone mother is enough of a problem."

While Deborah searches for housing, she finds out that several of the housing agencies have waiting lists as long as 15-20 years, and at the social housing agency she encounters discrimination, both as a foreigner and as a lone mother, describing the housing situation as "really terrible" with "all the bad apartments they give to people like me ... so when I get there they are really oppressive toward me ... and I'm not the only one who has experienced that". Deborah also finds that because she already has an education she is disadvantaged in terms of accessing help at the social centre:

> "I mean there are good and bad things about this system in Denmark for single mothers. The good thing is you have a place to live ... you're not on the streets, you have some money and you can more or less survive – but the bad thing is you cannot go above that, unless you try to get a degree or study ... and yet I'm not really supposed to do that because it's a kind of luxury to study while you're in the social system ... so for them it's a luxury that I'm studying and they have told me at any time they can say, 'There's a job for you, go out and work!' And I have said to them time and time again – I don't want low jobs, I have received a university education and I need to

get into another programme so I can move a step up so I can support myself and my daughter."

Deborah's isolation

Deborah feels isolated living in Denmark, without her family. She describes having a few "good friends ... who can help out", but the rest are "acquaintances". Since the break-up of her marriage she has not seen her parents-in-law, who cut off all contact and who she describes as having "a big grudge against me ... I'm the bad person in the family, the bad seed". Deborah's Danish husband is a successful professional, but has not assisted her in any way since the move and, despite his high income, pays only 1,200 Dkr a month for child support. Deborah's mother visited her in Denmark after Sarah was born, but she has not seen her mother or any of her family members since then, and Deborah is afraid to return home as she fears losing custody of Sarah. She also feels that Sarah has now developed an attachment to her father who spends more time with her now than he did when they lived together. Hence Deborah feels trapped – in order to remain with her daughter she must live in Denmark, yet she is in a precarious economic situation and at this point has not been successful in her application to receive §43, and reports that her social worker is unavailable and that "it takes days before I can get in touch with her". Deborah sees that the only route to her education is through SU and further huge loan debts, which will exacerbate her precarious financial situation for several years while her daughter is very young. She feels that as a foreigner she has had to fight for her rights at the social centre, where "basically you have to find out a lot of things about the social system in Denmark by reading, going to the library, and finding out – what are my rights?". Because she is a lone mother on social assistance, she feels she has been held in low regard, stigmatized by her treatment, and offered low-level short-term training, but no support for an education:

> "I'm running in a maze and if I don't do something to survive, I'm just going to blow up. I feel like it's useless. Nothing will get done and my voice will not be heard. Especially the fact that I'm a foreigner in Denmark."

Isolation and discrimination

The lack of integration in Danish society characterized most of the immigrant lone mothers' experiences. For the women who had stayed at Egmontgården, a community of lone mothers, some form of solidarity was established, but even there foreign women sought each other out almost as a buffer against rejection by Danish women. Adriana described her attempts at making friends, but concluded, "They talk to me nice but think I am different". In other cases cultural differences formed a basis for turning inward, as Zeinab chose to leave Boligfonden because of her disapproval of Danish permissiveness in child-rearing. When immigrant women were poorly educated and arrived in Denmark after meeting and marrying their Danish husbands in their native country, they were often trapped in negative circles of isolation. Such was the case of Carmina, who could not speak Danish well, did not know her rights, and was literally marooned in the countryside with no family, no network of friends, three young children and an abusive husband.

The ability to access the social services of the Danish social welfare system in turn depended on good assistance from social workers, and the ethnic minority women in this study have mixed reports; both helpful and indifferent social workers were encountered and the less education a mother had, the less she knew how to exercise her rights. In the case of Deborah who had received a degree in her native country and was fighting to obtain assistance under §43 to continue her education in Denmark, she concluded, "Basically you have to find out a lot of things ... – what are my rights?".

Maria, Deborah, Zeinab, Carmina and Adriana all describe varying degrees of racism based on their foreign status: Maria experienced several incidents on the public streets, where she was shouted at and told, "Go back to your own country", and was pushed by a man on a bus. These experiences were humiliating and debilitating and increased Maria's sense of vulnerability, causing her to stay home for days on end "afraid of going out and what will happen". Zeinab felt her former social worker did not like her and treated her badly, and she describes her as "a racist". Deborah reported that she encountered "really terrible" discrimination at the housing agency, with "all the bad apartments they would give to people like me". Carmina's story of violent taunts and abuse at the hands of her in-laws who forced her to pay 3 Dkr for coffee at their house, physically hit her, and offered to pay her to go back to her country as they did not want "no black girl" created enormous suffering for Carmina, a battered wife, who fled to a crisis centre with her three young children. She has been psychologically traumatized by her experience in Denmark, and apart from some assistance at the temporary crisis centre, has encountered indifferent treatment at the social centre, and is trapped in a cycle of no education, no prospects for her future, and is unable to leave the country with her children, as her ex-husband is currently fighting for custody. Adriana, on the other hand, who has experienced isolated ethnic insults on the streets and innuendoes from the health visitor who asked why her daughter "is so white", has a more optimistic view of her immigrant status: "Here it doesn't matter if you're Danish or not, they will help you". Of all the ethnic minority lone mothers in our study, Emilie appears to have made the most successful integration and wants to stay in Denmark rather than return to Greenland, stating, "I do not think of myself primarily as a Greenlandian person but as a human being like all others".

Custody rights and visitation

The area where immigrant lone mothers appeared to be most disadvantaged and badly treated was in relation to disputes over child custody and visitation, particularly in those situations of domestic violence by Danish husbands. For immigrant women married to abusive immigrant men, the violation of their rights appeared no different from that of their Danish lone mother counterparts, where battered women in general routinely experienced violations of their rights by the legal and police authorities (see Chapter 6). However, immigrant women married to Danish men experienced dual violations because they were not familiar with their rights, some were disadvantaged by their lack of fluent Danish, and all were unable to leave situations of domestic violence for 'home' because they were not permitted to take the children. So, fleeing domestic violence and returning to one's family was not an option, and joint custody arrangements resulted in Adriana losing custody of her son to her Danish ex-husband because she feared a confrontation and could not access help. In Carmina's case, she was traumatized by violent abuse, and felt that her lack of education, ignorance of Danish law and her poor Danish would all disadvantage her in court, where her violent husband was suing for custody while she lived at the crisis centre with her three young children. Carmina was the most severely traumatized of the immigrant women: she suffered acute anxiety attacks and depression. For ethnic minority women who had been victims of domestic violence, social isolation increased as they had to break tenuously formed networks in order to flee to safety, and once again begin alone with no friends or family in a new geographic area[1].

Social system supports for ethnic minority lone mothers

A paradoxical and positive set of policy practices appeared to operate in the lives of the ethnic minority lone mothers in our study. While they encountered random discrimination on the streets, and discriminatory treatment from housing officials, it appeared that they benefited from their outsider status in terms of support for an education. The differential racialization experiences that these lone mothers reported resulted in paradoxical effects; and there were great benefits for the women when social workers at the social centres supported their aspirations for an education. Whether it was because the social workers recognized and supported their obvious need of an education in order to make it in Danish society, or because they perceived ethnic minority women as a potential burden on the state and therefore saw it as necessary to push them into rapid economic self-sufficiency — was not always clear, but the outcomes for the women were, leading to a potential future of greater equality and independence. Maria received §43 to study as a social pedagogue, but knew of Danish women in similar situations at Egmontgården who were refused, saying, "Because I was a foreigner they thought it was a good idea — so it was not difficult for me to get it". Adriana, who has no formal education from her native country, has also been approved for §43, saying, "They really give you good help here in Denmark ... I want to become somebody". Zeinab has also been receiving educational support through §43 to complete her high school studies. In general, women who came from countries where support for lone mothers was minimal or non-existent appeared to have far more positive perceptions of the social support entitlements, and they viewed the Danish system as generous for lone mothers. As Adriana remarked, "... at home in my country they do nothing for lone mothers ...", and Maria corroborates this, saying, "Lone mothers in Denmark have a high status. They're protected".

While all of the mothers lived apart from their own families of origin, and encountered a lack of stable social networks that they could rely on for support, the one institution that appeared to offer stable and dependable support was the day care centre, where the children of immigrant mothers were welcomed and integrated into the fabric of their child community. For children caught in the maelstrom of family violence, the safe and alternative world at day care created strong social child networks which promoted resilience. For several of the mothers, the support offered by the pedagogues was a lifeline, and enabled them to pursue an education.

*   *   *   *

Immigrants in Western Europe: the broader picture

The experiences of immigrant lone mothers in our study must also be understood in the broader context of the status of immigrants in general in Denmark and Western and Northern Europe. Scandinavia has traditionally been far more hospitable to immigrants and refugees in comparison with other countries such as France, Germany, and Britain, but divisive and urgent problems of racism, social exclusion, and marginalization now confront Scandinavia and Western Europe, as right-wing parties and xenophobic ideologies have converged with many social democratic politicians to focus on restricting immigration. These heightened restrictions on immigration by governments of EU countries reflect common fears of 'overforeignization', which is perceived as threatening cultural and racial homogeneity and European identity (Jain, 1997). While in the post-war period immigrants were a source of cheap and much needed labour, globalization of the economy, high unemployment in many West and North European countries, and increasing numbers of refugees and immigrants have created a groundswell of popular sentiment to restrict immigration and avoid the high social costs of housing, welfare and education. As Sivanadan has pointed out, "What Europe wants is immigrant labour, not the immigrant" (quoted in Fekete, 1997). While in the 1960s and 1970s doors were wide open to foreign labourers, the political changes in Central and Eastern Europe in the 1990s, and the growth of asylum-seekers and undocumented immigrants have created hysteria in many countries about the "Islamic threat", "bogus marriages" and "claimants who want to take advantage of our welfare state but don't want to integrate" (Fekete, 1997, p 11).

Ethnic minorities in Denmark[2]

After the demand for foreign labour subsided and following the recession in the early 1970s, immigration policies were tightened and beginning in 1973, restrictions on immigration to Denmark were put in place. However, the 'immigration stop' (as it is called) does not apply to citizens from other Nordic countries and the EU. Hence immigrants from the EU and the Nordic countries enjoy special privileges compared with other nationals in terms of arrival and stays in the country. Other immigrants, the so-called 'third world' citizens, usually fall within the provisions of asylum, family reunification, workers with needed specialised skills and students[3]. Immigrants from 'third world' countries are predominantly from Turkey, Pakistan and Morocco, with the addition of more recent arrivals from the former Yugoslavia.

Since the mid-1980s a continuing debate on immigration has taken place in Denmark, focusing on integration and the high level of unemployment among immigrants that began during the economic recession. 'Foreigners' have frequently been made the scapegoats for societal problems by certain segments of Danish society.

In a 1990 Danish survey, 44% of the population believed that immigrants and refugees were the cause of Denmark's economic problems, and almost 50% believed that immigrants' rights should be restricted with Danes given priority in terms of the labour market (Jeppesen, 1995). In more recent years, the Danish National Institute of Social Research reports that Danish attitudes towards ethnic minorities seem to have developed in an even more negative direction. "Danes do not seem to have accepted the fact that they live in a multicultural society ... [and it is] especially the Muslim immigrants who are the object of Danes' antipathy" (Jeppesen, 1995, p 23). In the March 1998 Danish elections the anti-immigrant *Dansk Folkeparti* (Danish Peoples' Party) gained 7% of the vote and anti-immigration sentiments emerged as a key campaign issue.

In principle, while the laws of the country apply equally to all that live legally in Denmark, the 2000 Danish Alien's Act and the 1998 Danish Integration Act specifically apply to non-Danish citizens. In recent years there has been a great deal of attention by the Danish media and the Parliament to 'forced marriages' with particular concerns targeted at ethnic groups that engage in this alleged practice, which contradicts basic human rights. Provisions aimed at prevention of 'forced marriages' were introduced into the Danish Alien's Act of

---

31 May 2000. Act no 424 of the Danish Alien's Act no longer provides spouses under the age of 25 with a legal claim to unite in Denmark (Danish Board for Ethnic Equality, 2000). This has restricted the legal right of persons under the age of 25 (both foreign and Danish residents) to apply for residency under the family reunification provision[4].

Until 1999, immigrants and asylum-seekers had the same rights as Danes to health care, housing and social assistance, although their access has frequently been obstructed by lack of information. In addition, many immigrants experience housing discrimination which, coupled with high public housing rents, refusal of private owners to rent to immigrants and the inability of many immigrants to purchase their own flats or houses (Jeppesen, 1995) has created a 'ghettoization' of immigrants in concentrated public housing areas intermixed with Danes who have social problems. Social security rights are also threatened by regulations that require asylum-seekers and immigrants to demonstrate that they are becoming proficient in Danish in order to receive benefits. In Århus, for example, work requirements were imposed on refugees for 20 hours a week before being eligible for benefits. This mirrors the pattern of bureaucratic obstacles observed in other Scandinavian and Western European countries, where asylum-seekers who do not reside in assigned towns or attend language classes may have their benefits cut (Fekete, 1997). Most recently, the principle of equality in Denmark was drastically threatened by legislation passed in January 1999, that is, section 6-15 of the Danish Integration Act. According to this legislation, refugees received reduced introductory payments of social assistance for their first three years and had no rights to rehabilitation or work activation (Ejrnæs, 1999; Danish Board for Ethnic Equality, 2000). In addition, their rights to internally relocate were restricted, and those that moved without prior approval risked sanctions and withdrawal or reduction of payments. But in February 2000, following protests and pressure from local municipalities, Danish humanitarian organizations and the United Nations High Commissioner for Refugees, the legislation was changed and the previous equality that existed between Danish citizens and refugees in terms of social benefits was restored. However, during their first three years, refugees' rights to free movement within Denmark is still restricted.

Labour market discrimination also adversely impacts on immigrants and refugees in Denmark who experience higher rates of unemployment. The Act on Prohibition against Differential Treatment in the Labour Market (Act no 459, 12 June 1996) prohibits direct and indirect discrimination due to race, colour, religion, sexual orientation, national, social, or ethnic origin, but the burden of proving discrimination falls on the victim. A recent 1999 study conducted by the Danish Board for Ethnic Equality (www.nel.dk/english/ Percived.dis.htm) reports that a high percentage of ethnic minorities experience discrimination – being denied jobs they are qualified for – with the Lebanese, Turks and Somalis reporting the highest number of cases and Bosnians the least (48%, 36%, 34% and 17% respectively). Although the majority of ethnic minority citizens are employed wage-earners, relatively higher proportions are jobless in the country as a whole, with employment predominantly in unskilled areas. In addition, the proportion of salaried and skilled ethnic workers is much lower, and ethnic minority women have higher rates and longer periods of unemployment (Jeppesen, 1995).

While immigrant lone mothers in our study view day care centres and pedagogues in a positive light and appreciated the opportunities given to their children, nationally day care centres and afterschool care facilities and clubs are used far less by ethnic minority families (Jeppesen, 1995), thereby resulting in less social integration for the youngest children and less early intervention services if necessary. It is important to question whether cultural hegemony may play an exclusionary role – for example, at the day care centres observed in this study, Christmas was celebrated with elaborate rituals in the classrooms where Muslim and other ethnic minority children were present, but no corresponding rituals were observed for Muslim celebrations such as Ramadan, or Jewish festivals such as Hanukkah. To what extent does that create early forms of social exclusion in the child's world?

Lena Dominelli (1988, 1997) points out that social system professionals often harbour arrogant and racist assumptions about ethnic clients and that the lack of bilingual and bicultural social workers creates culturally insensitive services for ethnic women in Britain. This critique is applicable to Denmark where the health, welfare, day care and educational systems lack adequate representation of ethnic minority professionals, and professionals often demonstrate a lack of cultural awareness and cultural sensitivity (Skytte, 1997). In the lives of immigrant lone mothers in our study, daily 'micro-incidents' of racism are rife where "the unarticulated nature of racism makes it difficult for the majority of white people to see racism as an endemic feature of society permeating all aspects of it" (Dominelli, 1998, p 8). There is much to learn from the daily life problems encountered by the immigrant women we have profiled: Maria's experience of being pushed on the bus and screamed at, and Carmina's experiences of abuse by her in-laws, Adriana's experience of being ignored by the police because of being unable to speak "good Danish", and Zeinab's reports of a racist social worker.

These micro-encounters of racism speak to larger issues, and echo the re-emergence of racism on the political agenda of Europe, in which the majority of EC (European Community) countries are former colonial powers, and where a recent European Parliamentary Committee of Inquiry found a "growing strength of racism and xenophobia" (Jain, 1997, p 183). Fekete argues that "racism is debasing Europe's democratic tradition" (1998/99, p 194), and that Europe's progressive political traditions are undermined as the debate is redefined around the welfare state and the social and economic costs of immigrants. Clearly Denmark's commitment to an equality tradition with its history of universal social support policies for immigrants is now under fire as right-wing gains by the *Dansk Folkeparti* (Danish People's Party) and the threat of the *nye Danskere* (new Danes) assume a menacing presence in the public discourse, which entraps lone mothers in a dual marginality.

As we view the complicated worlds of the immigrant lone mothers in our study, we see that ethnicity, lone mother status, and gender all intersect to form a web of problems that relate to broader political and social patterns of discrimination in Danish society. The notable exceptions appeared to be post-secondary educational support for the mothers and day care services for their children, which created clear positive outcomes for such vulnerable families. However, for immigrant lone mothers caught in the turmoil of family violence, enormous hurdles remain, and the capacity to fight for their rights in terms of child custody is clearly undermined by their lack of 'systemworld' knowledge and the absence of ethnic minority experts to help them navigate the hazardous legal and social services terrain.

Domestic violence, which operates within a well concealed culture of silence in Denmark as in most other democratic nations, extends its reign of terror beyond ethnic minority women to Danish-born women where gender and patriarchy intersect to create a loss of rights despite strong democratic traditions and commitments to social equality.

In Part III, the lives of two Danish lone mothers who have been terrorized for years by violent men are portrayed, and the disturbing absence of legal rights and protections is analysed.

Notes

[The information for the notes below has been kindly supplied by Mandana Zarrehparvar, Danish Board for Ethnic Equality, January 2001.]

[1] The situation of ethnic minority women who leave their husbands because of domestic violence and who seek protection from the Danish authorities has created innumerable and complex problems, and many women find themselves perilously trapped. They have been unable to leave their husbands because of fear of reprisals and have often been forced to stay with their abusers. Furthermore, to leave one's husband and return to one's country of origin is often very problematic, because the women face lives of oppression in their own home countries. If the woman has not lived in Denmark for more than three years when she divorces her husband, her residence permit is cancelled.

[2] In Denmark ethnic minorities typically fall into two classification categories: *immigrants:* people born outside of Denmark, where both parents are foreign citizens or are born outside of Denmark; *descendants:* people born in Denmark, where neither parent is a Danish citizen born in Denmark. Officially the authorities use the terms *immigrants* and *refugees* to describe the group of people who come from 'third world' countries. Since the beginning of the 1990s it has become more common to use the term 'ethnic minority' to signal that the Danish society is multicultural and inclusive.

[3] Asylum and family reunification:
(a) apart from family reunification, the only other legal route to Denmark is through seeking asylum. Denmark is a signatory to the Geneva Convention of 1951 and abides by the asylum provisions. Furthermore, Denmark has also developed a *de facto* refugee status, that is, those who do not fall within the provisions of the Geneva Convention can be recognized as refugees if they are individually persecuted for reasons other than those mandated by the Geneva Convention, or if the authorities lack evidence but cannot exclude the possibility of persecution. People denied asylum have the right to appeal to the Minister of the Interior, who has the authority to grant a residence permit on humanitarian grounds. This only happens in very few cases, for example, if there is a humanitarian catastrophe in the country (eg Afghani women with children), or if the person is terminally ill.

In 1999 there were 6,530 spontaneous asylum-seekers in Denmark (ie those people who seek asylum after entering Denmark), the largest group being from Iraq.

A total of 4,223 people were granted asylum and 220 were granted a stay on humanitarian grounds.

Asylum-seekers come from a wide range of countries. The largest groups come from Afghanistan, Iran, Iraq, former Yugoslavia, Lebanon (mostly Palestinians), Romania, Somalia, Sri Lanka, Vietnam, Chile and Ethiopia.

(b) Family reunification provisions permit a spouse, registered partner or a common law husband/wife, infants or parents over the age of 60 years of a person living in Denmark (both Danish and foreign nationals), to be granted a residence permit provided that eligibility criteria are met. In addition, some ministerial discretion is available to grant residency to close relatives who do not meet the above criteria (although the conditions are more restrictive for foreign nationals). In 1999, 9,442 people were granted a stay on the basis of the provisions on family reunification with spouses comprising 65-70%.

[4] Prospective marriage partners have to prove that the marriage is based on their free will, the couple must have sufficient attachment to Denmark, and have secured an apartment (the last two conditions are also imposed on people over the age of 25). As a further condition a foreign national, irrespective of his/her age, they must also have the ability to support their spouse financially.

Part III:
Violence and the culture of silence

The impact of family violence

As we reflect on the linkages between social and economic vulnerability and violence among the women in our study, it is significant to note that 11 of the 20 lone mothers we interviewed were also victims and survivors of domestic violence. While we did not purposefully select women who had experienced domestic violence (only four were contacted through crisis centres), it was during the course of our qualitative interviews that the experience of domestic violence emerged as a central and traumatic theme of family life. Of the 14 life stories presented in this study, eight emerge engulfed by violence, and for four of the women, childhood abuse forms another layer of a violent life history.

What does life under siege do to economically vulnerable lone mothers, and how do they cope with their dual responsibilities as nurturers and providers for their children? How do they and their children live with the daily terrors of threats, assaults and violations of their selfhood? And, more importantly, how do the social and legal authorities perceive the situations of battered women and their children – as marital discord? As the couple's own problem to solve? Or as criminal behaviour and assault? As we listen to the following stories of Sanne and Lone – Danish women who have suffered extreme brutality at the hands of their male partners – and recall the experiences of Gina and Hanne in Part I, and of Carmina, Adriana, Emilie and Zeinab in Part II, it is clear that all these mothers have experienced varying levels of indifference and inaction from the police and the legal authorities, which were further exacerbated if the victims were ethnic minority women. In most situations chronicled in this book, the social authorities appear frequently neglectful of the women's needs and fail to recognize the traumatic impact of violence on their lives and the destabilizing effect on the family unit. The patriarchal bias that favours fathers' rights and the legal and social welfare presumption that the best interests of the children are served by ongoing contact with their fathers, irrespective of their violent behaviour, creates an ongoing

potential for danger in the lives of the women and children –
frequently placing their safety at risk when custody is shared or
visitation takes place. The impact on the children of witnessing their
mothers being battered and, in several cases, almost killed, appeared
to make little difference in custody or visitation agreements decided
on by the municipal authorities or the courts, and although some of
the fathers have also abused their own children, mothers have little
power to limit or prevent contact with violent, alcoholic or drug-
abusing fathers.

The gendered discourse that shapes legal and welfare policies
regarding domestic violence against women, as distinct from other
forms of 'stranger' violence, has a dramatic and disabling impact on
women and their rights as citizens and residents to protection from
the state. The impact of violence on the children who suffer as both
witnesses and victims is ignored in favour of the unchallenged
presumption that contact with violent fathers is better than no contact
at all, and ultimately serves the best interests of children. These issues
are explored further in the narratives of Sanne and Lone, whose life
stories are distinguished from the other women in our study because,
for them, brutal intimate violence has become the determining reality
of their lives as lone mothers – creating a landscape of terror which
overshadows all other experiences.

SIX

Life under siege

Sanne, Kasper and Michael

"And in November, we really had a crisis, it was very bad and I was full of bruises all over, and I really didn't get over that ... I don't know ... it was too extreme ... then when I left it was June, we couldn't stay when he was very violent ... I didn't have any alternative – I was afraid he was going to kill me!"

Twenty-nine-year-old Sanne has two sons, Kasper (four) and Michael (one). Sanne has experienced repeated violence from both fathers of her children. On many separate occasions Sanne has fled with her children to a crisis centre, only to return later to more violence and brutality. Sanne's own early childhood was scarred by abandonment when her parents divorced, and she lost all contact with her mother with whom she only reconnected again at the age of 21. Growing up with her father and stepmother, Sanne describes parental discipline as "hitting of the children but not beating". Sanne completed the 10th grade as well as a three-year commercial high school training.

Both the men that Sanne has been involved with as a young adult have been extremely violent – she is separated but not divorced from the father of Kasper – and she has until recently been living with Michael's father. Sanne speaks insightfully yet with a strange lack of emotion about the traumatic events of the recent past, and displays a passive almost dissociative response to her experiences of brutal abuse. Her current ground floor flat that she has just moved to from the crisis centre is pleasant and spacious, with two large bedrooms and a large living room; but Sanne remains concerned about a possible break-in from Michael's father from whom she fled several months earlier. However, despite these continuing fears, and her past history, Sanne feels powerless to prevent Michael's father from arriving unannounced to see his son.

Living with violence

Sanne describes years of physical and psychological abuse, beginning with her husband, Kasper's father, who used both drugs and alcohol. The violence began when she became pregnant with Kasper:

> "It could be anything. He would come in and he would be in a very bad mood and I could say something and he listened to it and he had a very bad temper ... he would hit me and then he threw me out ... it was just you know a beating ... and so when he threw me out when I was three months pregnant, I went to my doctor."

When Kasper was born the violence continued, as did the psychological abuse, so much so that Sanne felt she had no trust in herself, as her husband both terrified her and undermined her self-esteem, telling her constantly that she was insane, and that "he was going to break me down to build me up". She went to see a psychiatrist who told her that she was married to a psychopath, but still she received no support from any family members or from the social authorities to leave. She felt very isolated during this time, describing herself as "so ashamed", cut off from friends, and very afraid of her husband's rages.

After a traumatic incident when Sanne and Kasper were "thrown out" of the house, Sanne finally made contact with a crisis centre. Despite the violence of this last incident, Sanne still characterized her husband as "not extremely violent" and the experience as "not that bad ... my nose was all black but [laughs] he squished my nose and slapped me", although when he threatened the baby, she became aware of the danger:

> "I was sitting with the baby. I don't know ... I was feeding him ... and I was afraid he was going to harm him, so I went into the bedroom. And he took him out of my arms and threw him down on the bed, and that was the day I was very afraid he was going to harm the baby."

It was after this incident that Sanne went to the crisis centre, but after a month she returned to her husband, only to leave again 11 days later and return to the crisis centre, allowing her husband to keep all their possessions:

> "I didn't want to fight over a few things. I had my child and that was it. So that was why he kept everything ... I left the house and the

furniture and everything. He got everything and the car ... I didn't get anything."

In addition to losing her flat which was repossessed due to her husband's failure to make payments, Sanne inherited many debts from him, but describes herself as "not having the strength" to pursue this in court. She states she loved her ex-husband, he was like an "an obsession". After she separated from her husband, Sanne became involved with another man, who she describes as even more violent. By comparison with him, her former husband appeared "almost like a puppy". Sanne stayed with this man for almost two years although he too became violent early on in the relationship. She became pregnant and did not want a baby with him and had an abortion, but when she became pregnant a second time, she "didn't have the strength to go through another one [an abortion]". The baby, Michael, was born in August and in November Michael's father battered her and tried to strangle her; she was hospitalized with concussion and then fled back to the crisis centre with the children, later returning for another six months before finally leaving him: "Then when I left it was June, we couldn't stay when he was very violent ... I didn't have any alternative. I was afraid he was going to kill me".

Sanne, at this point, was living in a constant state of terror. She was afraid to call the police and expected little support as in previous situations she had been told that if she pressed charges, he would only receive a sentence of 2-3 weeks in prison. She carefully timed and planned her escape for when he left the house to buy some beer:

> "He said he was going to be there in 10 minutes or 15 minutes, so I just packed the children and I didn't even get their coats or shoes on them or anything ... called a taxi ... and said he had to be there in five minutes ... I just took the children. And then when I had been at the crisis centre for five days I really got a very very bad headache ... I'd never experienced anything like it. So at three at night I called the doctor, she came and said it was a concussion, but it could be worse, because it had taken so long for the symptoms to show. She said it might be a blood vessel so I had to go the hospital."

Sanne contacted a lawyer after this assault but again felt powerless, abandoned by the legal system which prescribes very light penalties for domestic violence, and by the continuing threat that Michael's father would continue to yield as he was legally entitled to visitation rights with his son, despite the dangers that that caused Sanne. After Sanne left the crisis centre and moved into her current flat he continued to visit. More violence took place when she took the children to visit him and he beat her in front of the children. This time he threw her out of his house and held the children hostage:

> "He threw me out without the children. I was not allowed to have the children with me, because he knows when I haven't got the children, I'm bound to go back. I have to have my children, I'm not going to leave them."

Sanne called a counsellor at the crisis centre for help; the police were summoned and escorted her back to the house where she fetched the children. Battered and bruised, Sanne relates, "I had to go the hospital because I felt my arm was broken and I had to fix my face", and she and the children once again returned to the crisis centre. There were no arrests as Sanne feared reporting the assault, acknowledging that, in this way, she "always protects him", and so the police took no action.

Since that time there have been no further incidents of violence but Michael's father continues to have unlimited access to her flat, pays no child support (with her compliance) and appears whenever he chooses without any prior arrangements or permission. Sanne continues to feel afraid although she states that she has set limits and asks him to leave if she feels threatened. She feels she has no power to prevent Michael's father from seeing him and yet continuing contact creates an ongoing threat. Sanne states:

> "Sometimes fathers have too much right to see the children, when it's not good for the children [with violent fathers] ... I mean it's up to the woman to prove that the father has been violent and how are you going to prove that six months later? You can't say that, you can't say look at my bruises if you haven't reported it to the police you can't really prove it. And if you can't prove it ... the lawyer I talked to said there was another thing I could do. She could write a letter to him pointing out he had been violent and she's going to give me a copy if he tries for custody."

While living under the sword of Damocles, Sanne also describes how she feels sorry for Michael's father: "I just feel pity for him ... he's had a bad life", as he too, grew up in a home filled with family violence and child abuse, "but it doesn't excuse what he's doing because I don't want my children to grow up the same way and become unhappy people". As she reflects on her own traumatic life over the past four years, she states that the crisis centre counselling has enabled her to develop some self insights and she is also seeing a psychologist to make sense of her attraction to such men:

> "[Violent men] are more exciting. You're never bored with a man like that. But in a way the excitement is, it tends to be a bit of a danger at the same time. You always live on the edge ... I wish I could feel anger at them now but I don't, only pity, I've learned a lot about myself, but ... it takes time to get over it, to accept it and to build up something new. Because I have to build up something new, otherwise I'll just end up in a relationship similar to the others."

Sanne expresses strong concerns about her two sons, Kasper and Michael. Kasper, who was four at the time of the initial interviews, has witnessed several assaults on his mother by both his own father, and by Michael's father. Kasper has also experienced multiple visits to the crisis centre as Sanne has fled to there on four separate occasions, first fleeing from the violence of Kasper's father and then from Michael's father. All of these assaults have occurred during very impressionable years for Kasper, and it appears that of the two boys he has been most affected by family violence. He has also been abused by his own father, with whom he has only sporadic contact. In the following section, Kasper's experiences are chronicled.

"And he was watching": Kasper's violent family life

Sanne describes how, after the incident when Kasper's father had thrown Kasper on the bed as an infant, she became very afraid that he would harm the baby, and that, "I just thought I didn't want him to grow up and become like his father". For Kasper and his mother that was the beginning of the traumatic cycle of battering, fleeing and returning, only to flee again. After Sanne finally left her husband when Kasper was still an infant, he had very infrequent contact with his father. However, when Kasper was two years old, he returned from an overnight visit with his father, and Sanne found bruises on him. She suspected that his father had beaten him but she did not report it until later in the week when she saw the doctor, who told her she should have reported it immediately, for proof. "Because I didn't bring him to the hospital the same day [the doctor] said it might as well have been me that had done it – so she said the next time [it happened] I should report it." Since that time Sanne has tried to avoid contact with Kasper's father and as the father is indifferent to his son, that has been possible. At this point Kasper has not heard from his father for over a year and Sanne states, "I didn't want to communicate with him again, because I didn't know what it was going to mean if I was going to contact him". Sanne also expresses concerns about what to do when Kasper gets older: "I also know when he's older, he probably wants to see him. I don't want him to, I want him to be stronger. I want him to know what's right and wrong".

When Sanne became involved with her new boyfriend "[he] started getting violent very early" and Kasper was witness to regular beatings and assaults of his mother during her pregnancy. Soon after Kasper's brother, Michael, was born, Kasper witnessed the brutal beating and attempted strangling of his mother by Michael's father. Several months later, Kasper, with his infant brother, experienced the terrifying ordeal of being held hostage by Michael's father for two hours after he broke Sanne's arm and threw her out of the house, and they were rescued by police intervention, and the family once more returned to the crisis centre. At this point Kasper, at three-and-a-half years old, had been the direct and vicarious victim of multiple forms of domestic terror and violence causing grave disruption and instability in his young life.

While Sanne has voiced anxiety about the impact on the children of frequent stays at the crisis centre, "it really affects the children to live in a place like that", she does not articulate similar concerns about the impact that witnessing violence may have had on the children, particularly on Kasper, although she acknowledges that Kasper "was watching" during the frequent episodes of violence. Sanne expresses other concerns about Kasper, describing him as "hypermobile", which she dates to the time he returned, at two years old, bruised, from visiting his father: "He keeps falling and he can't control it ... when he fell he didn't reach his hands, he just fell down and hit his head ... the therapist said that there was something wrong with his balance". Kasper has continued to see a physical therapist and the balance problem appears to have partially improved.

Observations of Kasper at home and at day care

Kasper, at four years old, is observed alone in the living room of his home with his mother and younger brother in adjacent rooms:

> Kasper is not reserved even though I [the male observer] am a stranger. It is very hard for him to keep still and calm for more than a few seconds, he is easily distracted and has only a brief attention span and he appears physically uncoordinated. For a short time he concentrates, but then crawls around the sofa again – standing on his head, hanging over the edge, or lying down. "Do you want to see what I can do – wrestling and karate?", he tells me as he talks constantly jumping from idea to idea as he shows me different things. His language is difficult to understand and appears somewhat delayed, but he talks non-stop wanting to communicate. He spends time drawing and first draws a body, head and eyes saying "that's a weird person" and then adding "that's also a dangerous person". He then draws a tiger but says, "it died" humming and very engrossed in drawing the stripes, which he colours yellow. The next drawing is fragmented and lacks any form or outline. Kasper announces, "that's the small animals ... Karius and Baktus". Soon he begins to create a fantasy: "There is fire everywhere and there's a gun that shoots". While he is drawing he interrupts his play to go out of the room to speak to his mother or to bring in additional objects; it is difficult for him to stay focused on the drawing activity.
>
> It appears from this observational visit that Kasper is insecure and hyperactive and Sanne confirms that he continues to have physical coordination problems as he is flat-footed and has weak joints. The physical therapist has suggested wrestling to strengthen his muscles. Kasper also has difficulty concentrating. The communication with me [the observer] is almost too friendly as I am a stranger, and he performs constantly to keep my attention as if he is afraid of losing the friendly contact. Kasper appears to have a somewhat chaotic picture of himself and his world as revealed by his drawings, which are very fragmented and indicate a developmental lag in the capacity to depict rudimentary representations of the human form.

Three months later Kasper's pedagogue is interviewed. She has known Kasper for the full two years that he has attended day care and is very supportive and sensitive to his developmental needs, saying:

"Earlier it was difficult for us to keep his attention but he has developed enormously [over the past two years] ... before he was a real troubled boy ... now he is very active and has always needed to run around and scream a little ... you must say he has some major inner resources to manage all the things he has been exposed to ... and he has come through it well ... his mother talks to him a lot about what has happened ... he doesn't go around being sad, he is not aggressive and now does not in any way show that he's having a hard time ... he doesn't show signs of anxiety – he is a strong boy and the other children look up to him ... they want very much to play with him – he has a small group of three to four boys that he belongs to and they miss each other when one is away ... he is very helpful to the younger children, very sensitive and concerned ... and he likes to comfort and touch them."

The pedagogue's overall assessment of Kasper is that he has motor-coordination problems but that his social and language development appear to be normal. She points out that he has never been good at creative activities, but that she sees his strengths in his play which is very active, and remarks, "If I came to visit without knowing him I would not notice that he has had problems". Three months later, when Kasper has turned five, he is observed at the day care in February 1998:

They are having lunch when I arrive around 11 o'clock. Kasper does not recognize me from the home observation as it is over six months ago. Kasper eats calmly, puts his lunch box on the table and the pedagogue reminds him that he has dropped some food. Kasper picks up the bread and throws it away and comes back to the table. He takes his cup, and seemingly without any provocation, throws some of the milk on another child's head, who becomes angry and a little later the same child takes his cup and throws the milk on Kasper's head. They get mad at each other but do not really fight, and soon a pedagogue separates them, asking Kasper to pick up his bread which he does. Kasper sits at the table, chatting and shouting with the same boy. Suddenly he stands up, takes the stool in his hands and lifts it threateningly above his head – but he does not do anything further and sits down again. A little while later there is a birthday celebration for Louis. A chair is placed in the middle of the room which Louis sits on and all the children sing a birthday song, with Kasper participating. He appears calm, sits on the stool, with sudden random outbursts of shouting which surprise the other children. Later the children are playing outside – Kasper runs around wildly participating in a play activity which involves collecting boxes which they build up in front of the entrance to the play house. After some time Kasper and another boy run out of the play house, Kasper grabs him and says, "We'll also make a dungeon here – you are going inside the house". The other boy objects but Kasper directs him. Now they are playing in two play houses beside each other which have become dungeons. Kasper says, "Look this is a real dungeon", but the other child is not interested, saying, "I have my own", which Kasper accepts, saying, "Then you can come and visit me". The two boys then play cooperatively and are joined by other children, as they continue to be very engaged in their fantasy play which continues for about 30 minutes until the two boys join a war game that begins outside with one of the male pedagogues.

The overall impression of Kasper at the day care centre is that he is independent, aggressive, but well-integrated into the group life at the centre. He has made many friends and is liked by the other children. The day care observations are a striking contrast to the drawings and home observations conducted six months earlier, which revealed a different emotional level of functioning, and perhaps some deeper psychological anxieties. The day care staff appear very supportive of Kasper, and it appears as if the centre has provided an island of stability. In this institution he has succeeded in establishing positive relationships with other adults (including the male pedagogues), and the day care centre provides an alternative social world for this five-year-old child, who has endured multiple traumatic experiences of violence in his young life.

Sanne: coping alone with her children

Sanne lives in a very isolated world, she appears to have few friends and no network of informal supports. Her father and stepmother are not supportive and while Sanne describes her newly formed relationship with her biological mother in positive terms, she does not appear to receive much practical help from her. On the two occasions when we interviewed Sanne, she was ill, suffering from pneumonia, but continued to catch the bus with Kasper to day care and to take care of Michael with no other adult to assist her. The only visible point of continuing support has been the crisis centre, which also serves as her ultimate refuge. She describes the crisis centre as "really helpful ... you can get help there ... but you have to want it ... they don't force you". It was the crisis centre that helped Sanne locate her current flat and the crisis centre counsellor, whom she called in desperation, when her children were held hostage by Michael's father. Sanne attends group counselling at the crisis centre once a week and is also seeing a psychologist. She appears depressed and describes herself as "not really good at receiving help" and too "embarrassed ... and ashamed" to have confided in any family member or friends that she was a victim of ongoing male violence. She feels stigmatized by the fact that she was twice a victim, stating that "people don't see that it's not my fault". When Sanne contemplates taking any legal action against Michael's father who battered her so brutally, or thinks about establishing contact with friends, she describes herself as "too tired" and "not having the strength for it".

Sanne, who had co-owned her home with her husband, lost everything when she fled to the crisis centre, and as he did not make the payments on the flat, it was repossessed and auctioned. She has also inherited large debts from him and states that she does not have the strength to go to court about it, nor has she been willing to press charges against Michael's father, saying she was afraid because he has continuing access to Michael. Afraid and pressured she has also signed away her right to child support from Michael's father, "because he bought a very big apartment", and as she has given her permission for non-payment, she does not receive child support.

At present Sanne feels that she can manage financially on social assistance combined with the housing subsidy she receives for her flat, as well as free day care for Kasper, and she is now waiting for a place to open up for Michael. She hopes to continue her education when Michael begins day care and her former social worker has encouraged her to pursue post-secondary education. She needs one more year of high school as preparatory education before applying for admission to psychology at the university. However, Sanne is aware that there have been work activation policies instituted for lone mothers, and while she hopes that she will be eligible for §43, she fears that she may be refused "because they've done a lot of changes".

Sanne and her children in the future

Sanne appears to suffer from many symptoms of post-traumatic stress disorder syndrome. She is chronically tired and appears passive and dissociative in discussing the violence she has been subjected to at the hands of her sons' fathers, both of whom have threatened her life on numerous occasions. She is isolated socially and receives little or no help from the Danish legal system, and she feels it is futile to even try. She says she feels no anger toward these two men who have assaulted her, but rather feels "pity" and identifies with their own backgrounds of childhood abuse. While she is now seeing a psychologist to try and cope with her past, she continues to feel threatened by the ongoing presence of Michael's father in the life of her child, and the control that he continues to exert by visiting Michael at her flat whenever he chooses.

In terms of facing the future, Sanne is aware she has hit rock bottom, saying, "Well they [things] can't get any worse". She continues to experience shame and embarrassment about the violence and what has happened to her, and feels stigmatized because she believes other people see her negatively. Both the crisis centre and the day care centre have been pinnacles of refuge and stability for Sanne and her children, all of whom are vulnerable in the face of potential further violence by Michael's father. It is also clear that while Sanne has not yet developed the strength to confront her past, nor to create boundaries of protection for herself and her children, her problems are compounded by a police and court system that view violence against women and children with indifference, instituting weak sanctions for the perpetrator. Furthermore, the emphasis in the legal system on fathers' rights – even violent fathers' rights – to see their children, creates ongoing security risks for women like Sanne, as their own rights as mothers are compromised when they are forced to confront physical danger and domestic terror as part of the price for separation or divorce from violent men.

Lone, Jesper, Michelle and Peter

> "[After the violence] I decided to leave him and went to a town far from our home. I just wanted to get away from everything.... I took the baby and our clothes ... I did not know anybody there.... First I stayed at a crisis centre, but then I got help to get an apartment....

> Kenneth did not know where we were living.... But after two years
> I missed my own family very much and moved back."

Twenty-six-year-old Lone is the mother of six-year-old Jesper and
three-year-old Michelle, and has just given birth to Peter, who is
three months old. Jesper and Michelle are the children of Lone's
abusive former partner from whom she has suffered chronic and
unremitting abuse.

A young mother living with violence

When Lone and Kenneth met, Lone was 18 years old and was
attending school to become a chef's assistant, and Kenneth, at 27,
had a good job working for an automotive centre. Lone described
him as "a very good, nice, and careful man" at the beginning of their
relationship. Soon Lone was pregnant and when Jesper was born,
Kenneth changed completely. He started drinking heavily and
became violent towards Lone. He was jealous of the baby, and he
wanted Lone's attention all the time. After he repeatedly assaulted
her, Lone left and moved to another area but two years later she
returned, as she felt isolated and alone living far away from her family.
After moving back home, Lone made contact with Kenneth as she
"still had many feelings for him at that time. I thought, OK, Jesper
needs a father and I need a man. Then I took him back".

When Jesper was two years old, Lone and Kenneth moved into
a flat close to Lone's parents. Lone and Kenneth had their second
child together, and soon after Michelle's birth, Kenneth started his
abusive behaviour again, screaming, shouting and again becoming violent
towards Lone. Lone believed that he was mentally ill and once again
she decided to leave him. This time Lone moved with Jesper and
Michelle to a local crisis centre where they lived for the next seven
months before moving into a flat on their own. But life at their new
flat has been fearful, as Kenneth has continued to stalk and assault
Lone, and they live under constant threats of his ongoing violence:

> "He makes trouble all the time.... He kicked the door in and smashed
> everything.... When I go into town he runs after me and screams at
> me.... He banged my head against the toilet and I was bleeding, and
> the ambulance came.... He hit me and smashed my teeth.... Jesper
> remembers this very, very clearly.... Kenneth sometimes sits drinking

and screaming outside of Jesper's kindergarten.... I have a mobile telephone with me now so they can 'phone me the moment Kenneth wants to go and get Jesper.... He also hit Jesper.... I have only called the police once, and when I did Kenneth got very angry. He was sentenced and had to go to jail for it.... My neighbour has seen him kick my door in, but he would not testify in court because he is afraid of Kenneth."

Despite Kenneth's uncontrolled violence, and the publicly witnessed verbal and physical abuse towards Lone and Jesper, he still maintains joint custody of his son. Lone is very concerned about the impact of the violence on Jesper and about the time he spends with his father as she notices that his behaviour changes and he becomes very upset whenever he sees him. After he returns from a visit, Jesper often aggressively destroys toys in his room, cries, hits his mother and tells her that he is angry. Lone recounts an exchange with Jesper after he returned from one visit with his father and Jesper told her, "Mother, you should have a knife in your back ... because you don't love my father". Lone also has concerns that Jesper's paternal grandmother contributes to the unhealthy and psychologically damaging environment that Jesper's father creates, trying to turn him against his mother. Lone describes her sense of powerlessness: "I feel like a lost mother, and there is nothing for me to do when my children are set against me".

Battling for custody

Lone has tried to limit Jesper's contact with his father, and she has demanded that Kenneth's mother supervise Jesper's visits with his father. However, Lone is also uneasy and worries constantly about the children's safety when Kenneth's mother supervises their visits because Jesper's grandmother has herself lived in a very violent relationship with Kenneth's father who abused her and Kenneth during Kenneth's childhood. In the past Kenneth's father would terrify them by shooting a gun out of the windows of their home. While Kenneth currently has shared custody of Jesper (but not of Michelle), Lone is trying to gain sole custody of Jesper, and the case is winding its way through the court system, which is a slow process. Lone has been told that Kenneth's violence towards her and Jesper will probably not influence the court's decision about custody, that as long as Kenneth tries to keep in contact with them and is not abusing drugs, the outcome of her custody battle remains unsure.

Hence Lone's rights to a life free from violence are given little attention in the court system; rather, her behaviour is placed under question: "[At court] they said, if the man is violent, then what have you said to him? It is no use ... I am so small against everybody else". However, despite the lack of attention paid to Kenneth's violence, Lone has some grounds for optimism that a verdict will go in her favour because Kenneth has publicly demonstrated his "unfit" status as a father by appearing at court hearings intoxicated, and he has a long history of an unstable and damaging relationship with Jesper which has caused Jesper considerable pain and rejection.

Jesper: a childhood of fear and turmoil

"Jesper does not understand anything, and [he says], 'Daddy is not speaking nicely about you, Mom'. And it is very hard to explain to him.... And he asks me, 'Why do we have to see him?' And I tell him, 'Because he is your father'. And Jesper cannot accept that Kenneth and I cannot speak together. It makes him very confused.... At the preschool class they found out that Jesper was very sad because his father and mother don't speak together like grown-up people. That is why Jesper is always thinking and thinking and thinking. He cannot understand it. At his school, when somebody speaks loudly, he gets frightened, and he shows it by becoming very violent to me because he is angry with me."

Jesper has also experienced many occasions during his young life when he has felt abandoned by his father who has a history of not showing up for scheduled visits. In the past Lone would make excuses for Kenneth and try to protect Jesper, but no longer:

"It is not me who is making a problem for Jesper. I am too soft with him. I have got to be harder on him. I have to tell him the truth about his father ... that something has happened and then why it has happened.... And [in the past] when Kenneth didn't show up [when he was supposed to], I always told Jesper that maybe his father had a new job or something.... So when he is with Kenneth, Jesper cannot go on believing the explanation I have given him. Then Jesper believes that I am lying to him, and he gets angry with me. So I am now going to tell the truth.... 'Maybe your father is coming; maybe he is not coming'."

Jesper is observed during a visit to his home:

> Jesper reacted with apprehension and wariness towards me [the male observer] and seemed frightened. He hid underneath his bed and would only come out when coaxed. It was difficult for me to have much contact with him, because he often disappeared from the room. When Lone asked Jesper to come back into the room, he refused, and when she asked him why he would not come back, Jesper said, "He is not a proper man". Lone asked him to explain what he meant, and Jesper answered, "He is not a pedagogue". His behaviour in this situation seemed to indicate insecurity and uncertainty about a stranger, and a need to know and categorize a new and unfamiliar male in his environment – who might constitute a possible threat.

Ann, the crisis centre psychologist, is a crucial support for Jesper, and she helps Jesper work through his anger and turmoil. On one occasion she described how Jesper drew a picture of a dinosaur with a big tongue and long nails crushing the wall. When she asked Jesper why he drew that picture, he told her, "Because my father hit my mother and I want to crush him with the tongue". There are also other adults at his school-age child care centre with whom Jesper feels comfortable, and from whom he can get some support for his difficult emotional life, and there is a psychologist at the pedagogical counselling clinic who is available. Jesper's pedagogues described him as a bright boy who has fun playing with and teasing the other children. But, they reported, it is difficult to engage Jesper over a longer period of time. Although he has better control of himself than he did a year ago, he is still very sensitive and fearful and his world easily falls apart. He is observed sitting stone-faced when he does not want to talk, and while the pedagogues feel that they have a good relationship with him, they often find it impossible to connect and fathom what he is feeling and thinking.

In his school classroom, Jesper receives little encouragement or support. He does not like his school at all, and a written report from his teacher contained few positive words about him. According to his teacher, Jesper has difficulty concentrating, he often leaves the classroom suddenly, his behaviour is disruptive, and he has learning difficulties. Jesper's problems in school appear symptomatic of post-traumatic stress disorder, yet he receives no interventions to support him during this acute and turbulent period in his young life.

A small circle of support

Throughout Lone's ordeal of chronic family violence, her social network has diminished. She rarely meets with friends of her own, and she spends most of her time alone with her children. Besides her constant fear and struggle to find a way to survive the ongoing violence, Lone and her children have been deeply affected by the recent sudden death of Lone's father. Lone was close to her father and is shaken by his death:

> "My father was a very good man. He visited me often after work and gave me a push to be happy. He never hurt my mother, but always looked at her as the woman he really loved. He did not like Kenneth and was very sad when I got pregnant with Jesper. He wanted me to go out sailing to see the world. He told me that Kenneth was a violent man ... and he told me many other things which I can see are right today. Jesper and my father were very close, and Jesper looked at my father as a father. Everything Jesper has to help him become a good man he got from my father. When my father died, Jesper changed a lot."

Since her father's death, Lone and her mother have become closer, and Lone's mother tries to help Lone as much as possible with the children, although she herself works as a secretary. Recently, Lone endured another experience of loss and rejection. She became involved with a boyfriend during the ongoing violence with Kenneth and became pregnant with his child. While initially the relationship felt good, Brian was arrested and spent two months in jail.

> "And when he came back [from jail], he was a very strange man here in the house. He was angry. Not violent, but angry and sad, and he didn't want to talk to me anymore. He wanted to be in his own world.... So his mother wanted me to know that Brian was on heroin. He smoked heroin, yes. He got very angry.... I said he should get some help to get off it, and he didn't want to do that, and then he moved.... So it is better for him to move than to stay here on drugs."

Brian left Lone four months before Peter was born. He has only seen Peter once, and has had no other contact with his infant son. Lone described how she became very anxious after Peter was born:

"I breastfed him for only one month. I was very stressed, and I thought the whole world was against me. Soon I stopped giving milk.... When I found out I had to live alone with the three kids, I got very frightened".

A steadfast support for Lone throughout her many ordeals is Ann, the psychologist at the private crisis centre. Ann has helped Lone deal with her fear and anger and her feelings about her violent relationship with Kenneth and her concerns about her children. Lone is very appreciative of Ann's support, saying, "She told me a lot of things I should try. She has opened me so I can speak [about my experiences]. Before I was closed in and I got very angry. I could not cry ... and then I became as hard as a stone". Ann also accompanies Lone to the social centre each time she goes there to meet with her social worker. Lone feels very bitter toward her social worker, who she feels mistreats her:

> "I want Ann to listen every time, so I have a witness to how they treat me.... They look at me like I'm a fool, yes, an idiot.... I get very angry. I am a person. Don't look at me because I am on social assistance and don't look at me because I have been beaten. I am another person, now, so please help me not to fall back to that and give me a push. She [the social worker] gives me no support, none. She is a crazy person.... I don't want to talk to her alone."

Because Lone's relationship with her social worker at the social centre is so bad, she avoids any direct contact with her whenever possible. A home help assistant from the social centre is assigned to Lone to assist her in taking care of her three young children. The assistant is supportive and is on call day and night, whenever Lone needs her. Lone also asks the home help assistant to carry messages and questions to the social worker so that Lone does not have to meet with her alone.

The future for Lone and her children

Lone manages to make ends meet on social assistance, but she would like to earn her own money and become self-sufficient and move to a flat in a better area. Many people with drug problems have moved in around her, and Lone feels that Kenneth and his violence have destroyed her reputation. Lone spends nearly all of her time alone with her three children, and feels extremely stressed and trapped by her situation:

"Everything I do is children, children, children, children.... Sometimes I say 'shut up', and it is not good, of course, but so many things have happened. And I do not have time to sit down and be myself and think about things.... I am not finished with all these things [that have happened in my life]. Maybe they will appear again later, but I must have time to work my problems out, so that they will not become like a bomb [inside me] and explode later."

She feels that a 'weekend family' every third week for Jesper and Michelle would help them all, and the children could benefit from having an adult male around, especially Jesper. Lone has been waiting a year already, and there has been no offer about a 'weekend family' from the social centre. Lone would like to complete her education as a chef's assistant when Peter is a little older, but feels helpless as her present situation overwhelms her:

"They always talk about me having an education; you've got to have this, you've got to have that. But what am I going to do with my children when they are sick, if they have a fever for four days and I've got to stay home when I should be in school?... You cannot take them out and so you get stuck at home with them."

When Lone thinks about her future, she is enveloped by the here and now demands of her three small children, and she is particularly concerned about what will happen to Jesper. She does not yet know the outcome of the custody case and wonders how she can support Jesper so he can recover and work through all of his traumatic experiences at the hands of his father. If he continues to stay at his present school, where his serious emotional needs and cognitive impairments are neglected, he will continue to be a 'problem child'. As a vulnerable and traumatized six-year-old, Jesper is clearly in need of focused pedagogical support and intensive interventions, and may indeed benefit from attending a school for children with special needs.

As Lone looks to the future, the horizon appears bleak. For almost eight years she has been terrorized by violence from Kenneth. The violence has overwhelmed her daily existence and that of her oldest son, rendering her powerless in the face of inaction by the police and the legal authorities. She has been indifferently treated by her social worker at the social centre and made to feel ashamed and an "idiot", undermining her fragile sense of self. If not for the emotional and practical support from the private crisis centre, where she has found refuge many times over the past years, her fragile family world may well have faced collapse. If Lone is to be helped to attain a more positive and stable future she will need a comprehensive and strong support system over an extended period which addresses the fears, the humiliations, and the violations she has suffered as a victim of domestic violence. Most importantly, her rights to a life free of terror and violence will need to be assured by a legal system that works to protect her and recognize the irreparable harm that domestic violence causes both mother and children.

The failure to tie male violence to parental 'fitness' places lone mothers in a dangerous netherworld of terror, stripping them of their rights as mothers to protect their children. The culture of silence that fails to recognize the gendered nature of the crime is pervasive: extending to schools, the courts, the police and the social welfare system. And it is vulnerable women such as Lone and Sanne who become 'lost mothers' as a consequence.

Patriarchy and the violations of rights

Increasingly, domestic violence is emerging as a central focus of the research on child abuse and family dysfunction, and reflects a developing awareness that domestic violence is a topic of major significance, as it raises interdisciplinary issues of concern that impact on the child welfare, public health, legal, social work, criminal justice and educational fields. It requires a shift in cultural perceptions and practices to no longer accept violence as an acceptable form of social control over women and children (Walker, 1989; Ford et al, 1995). Men who have been socialized to believe that they have the right to control the women in their lives are frequently men who have grown up with violence. While social conditions such as unemployment and poverty may under certain circumstances increase the likelihood of substance abuse, exacerbate family stress, and act as precipitating factors for violence, the two greatest risk factors for men who batter women are childhood experiences of witnessing their fathers or other men battering their mothers, or having been abused themselves during childhood (Hotaling and Sugarman, 1986). While beating children is now illegal in both Denmark and Sweden, in practice that same right and protection is not enforced in relation to women and partner violence. In our study there were eight cases of severe assaults requiring hospitalization but no corresponding arrests. There was also one case of attempted murder (for reasons of confidentiality this case was not included in the book) which was brought to the courts but failed to secure a guilty conviction due to lack of witnesses despite the mother's severe injuries. She has moved six times in the past four years and she and her children now live in terror of future attacks as her ex-husband continues to stalk and threaten her.

In Denmark, the law now categorizes domestic violence as a crime, but large gaps exist between the law and its implementation. This is even exemplified by the way in which domestic intervention by the police is classified – as *husspektakel* (house-noise) – a linguistic marker of the trivialization of the crime. For women living with violent men, changes in the criminal law since 1989 now place the onus on the police to take up the case against the batterer under §244, 245 and 246, but the punishment if arrests and convictions are made range from fines to a mere four years in prison, irrespective of the often severe and unremitting physical and psychological brutality. '*Tilhold*' (injunctions) can only be obtained after a woman has left her husband or partner and only if they do not share joint parental authority of the children. Prior to 1989 women had to be legally separated before they were permitted to seek an injunction, and in 1988, of 1,687 injunctions sought, only 393 were awarded throughout Denmark (Hester and Radford, 1996). In their cross-national study of domestic violence in Denmark and England, Hester and Radford point out how the procedures for obtaining injunctions in Denmark fall within the domain of the police (§265 and §266 of the criminal law), and that in practice the police routinely fail to issue the injunctions because they claim that there is a need for ongoing contact between the father and his children. In some areas of Denmark, the police are still applying the now defunct 'legal separation rule'. Even when injunctions are issued against men for stalking, harassment, or using physical violence to gain access, the sentences for violating injunctions are extremely light, ranging from fines to six months in prison.

In our study, many women expressed their sense of powerlessness in the face of weak protections and enforcement measures from the police and courts (see also Hansen and Østvand, 1998). As Gina, one of the women in our study, described the typical police response after she was severely assaulted by the father of her daughter, "They told him, you get out of this house now. If you don't get out we will take the children and put them in a home." This response appears to corroborate the findings of Hester and Radford, where women reported similar patterns of response and non-arrest by the police to situations of family violence: "The police see as their main role the calming of the perpetrator and protection of any children ... in practice the police may remove a violent man only if he is drunk or may otherwise take the abused partner and her children to a refuge" (Hester and Radford, 1996, p 57). Hence it is disturbing to note that the male perpetrator of violence emerges with few, if any, sanctions, retaining his rights of access to the children and frequently to the residence. It is the mother and children who must flee to a crisis centre, experience the loss of home and possessions, and the destabilizing and traumatic effects of both the violence and its aftermath. The lack of rights of women in the face of male violence and their inability to secure equitable treatment from police and the courts raises very strong concerns about the meaning of 'equality' and social citizenship rights in Denmark for victims of domestic violence. In our study Lone and Sanne suffered long-term ongoing violence and in Hester and Radford's study all the Danish women interviewed suffered severe ongoing experiences of violence – 15 of the 26 described the violence as continuing for nine years – and all experienced a variety of brutal assaults (broken bones, strangulation, rape, and sexual assaults) at the hands of their children's fathers. The failure of the authorities to understand the gravity of the situation, the failure to protect the rights of women, and the paucity of research in this area, points to the trivialization of this social problem within the culture, where domestic violence is viewed as a social welfare problem rather than as a crime. Denmark is, of course, not alone in failing to confront domestic violence as a serious social problem that threatens women's basic human rights.

In Britain, findings from the British Crime Survey reveal that 1 in 10 women living with a male partner experience domestic violence, 36% of violent incidents happen after separation takes place, and other recent findings indicate that the actual incidence of violence may in fact be much higher (Mirrlees-Black, 1995; Hester and Radford, 1996). In the US it is estimated that between two and four million women are battered each year by their male partners, and domestic violence is the largest single cause of injury to women (Straus and Gelles, 1990; McClure, 1996). In Canada the statistics are similar: 1 in 10 women is the victim of assault by her male partner (National Clearinghouse on Family Violence, 1991). However, domestic violence is also significantly underreported – in the US it is estimated that only 1 in 7 assaults is actually reported to the police (National Clearinghouse for the Defense of Battered Women, 1994); hence the actual incidence of domestic violence is assumed to be much higher.

The physical and psychological impact of violence against women

Lenore Walker's landmark study, *The battered woman* (1979), examined the physical and psychological impact of living with family violence, leading to the formulation of the 'battered woman syndrome' which increasingly came to be used in legal defense of women who killed their batterers, and to explain 'the learned helplessness' and apparent complicity of women who remained in the violent family, or failed to protect their children from abuse (Walker, 1979, 1989). Women who remain with their batterers are often characterized as 'trapped' in their relationships by a variety of economic and psychological factors. These economic factors vary depending on the availability of a social safety net. In the US for example, it is estimated that over 50% of homeless women and their children become homeless as a result of domestic violence, and in some communities the prevalence may be as high as 90% (Bassuk et al, 1996). Since the passage of new welfare legislation in the US in 1996, which drastically cut the social safety net, it is anticipated that this will further trap victims of domestic violence in violent households (Polakow, 1997). In Denmark, where public social resources are available and where women and children are provided with a social safety net, this problem differs dramatically from the US and also from the UK. Hester and Radford (1996) point out that Danish women, in contrast to their English counterparts, had greater access to a better resourced welfare state which created more favourable survival outcomes for them and their children. Hence it is clear that in a stronger social welfare state, such as Denmark, where women do not need to fear chronic homelessness and destitution, choosing to leave their abuser may become a more viable survival option. However, the psychological toll of self-blame, low self-esteem, depression and post-traumatic stress disorders may continue to trap women in cycles of powerlessness (Herbert et al, 1991), and legally mandated child contact may serve to place the woman in an ongoing relationship of threat and violence even after she leaves (Hester and Radford, 1996).

In relationships where domestic violence exists women are also at risk for numerous health problems, and between one quarter to one half are sexually and physically abused (Campbell, 1986; McClure, 1996). Numerous researchers cite pregnancy as a frequent trigger for battering, which places the fetus at risk for miscarriages, stillbirths and premature delivery, and the pregnant woman is more likely to be struck in the abdomen causing placental or fetal injury (Bohn, 1990; Hester and Radford, 1996). Women who are battered during pregnancy demonstrate symptoms of anxiety, depression, drug and alcohol use and decreased prenatal care (McClure, 1996). Other US studies point to consistent health problems that characterize battered women in general: insomnia, headaches, gastrointestinal symptoms, pelvic, back, and chest pains, and depression, suicide and drug and alcohol abuse (Amaro et al, 1990).

Danger points and escalation of violence: leaving and child contact

When women leave their batterers, they place themselves at increased risk of assault and homicide in the immediate period following the departure (Jones, 1991). In the US about 75% of battered women's visits to emergency rooms at hospitals occur after separation, and 75% of calls by women to law enforcement authorities occur after separation from batterers. In addition, women are at greater risk of homicide after they leave or when they inform the batterer they are leaving. In two separate studies conducted in different regions of the US, between one quarter and one half of homicides of women by male partners occurred during or immediately after separation (National Clearinghouse for the Defense of Battered Women, 1994). In Britain, findings from the Crime Survey indicate that 36% of violent incidents take place after separation by the woman from her partner (Mirrlees-Black, 1995). In their cross-national study of England and Denmark, Hester and Radford's findings (1996) indicate that in both countries the majority of women in their sample suffered continuing violence and abuse by their husbands or partners after they left the relationship. In our study, half of the women who experienced domestic violence continued to be assaulted once they left the relationship.

One of the continuing sources of danger for women who leave the relationship is the emphasis by legal and social welfare authorities on maintaining contact between the batterer and his children. One of the presumptions of child welfare and the courts is that the best interests of the child are served by attempting to maintain the parental relationship with the father. However, contact places the woman at risk for further assault and frequently makes her an ongoing victim of her former partner. Numerous US studies document threats, intimidation and assaults against women that are linked to visitation or custody arrangements of their children, particularly in circumstances involving the pick-up or return of children (Shepard, 1992; Edelson, 1995). Hester and Radford report all the assaults experienced after separation were linked to child contact arrangements. In both England and Denmark, the violence against the women was worsened in relation to leaving and continuing child contact, and the women were frequently left unprotected and alone in managing child contacts because professionals either failed to take domestic violence into account or minimized it. Hester and Radford found few instances of successful violence-free contact, and the focus of professionals consistently favoured securing parental agreement about the children and joint parental authority stressing the importance of the father–child relationship; although little attention appeared to be paid to the quality of the parenting relationship. The vast majority of fathers in their study were frequently drunk, emotionally or physically abusive to the children, and violent to the mothers in the children's presence after separation took place. Women, because of the unequal power caused by the fear of physical threats and assaults, were unlikely to challenge joint parenting arrangements.

In our study, all the women who had been victims of domestic violence, whether they had joint or sole custody, were obligated to permit their children ongoing contact with their fathers. In one situation the children were held hostage, and the mother was violently assaulted by the man who has maintained coercive access to her and to their son; in another case, the door of one lone mother's flat was broken down by her ex-husband and she was brutally battered and her head smashed on a concrete floor while her son watched, yet she was still required to maintain child contact with the father through visitation, and was unsure whether she would receive sole custody after the attack. One of the immigrant mothers had joint parenting but lost her son to her abusive Danish husband who arranged for the child to live with him and his grandmother one year after the divorce, and she felt powerless to challenge him. She was told by the authorities that they had nothing to say about joint custody arrangements between parents – it was up to them to work out their differences. As one Danish attorney remarked, joint parental authority is about "the right of the strongest" (Hester and Radford, 1996, p 43).

Despite accumulating evidence in the US, Britain and Denmark that contact in custody and visitation arrangements places women at risk for future assaults, child welfare authorities and the courts have been reluctant to question the rights of violent fathers to maintain relationships with their children, or to consider the presence of domestic violence in deciding custody and visitation arrangements. This presumption that 'any father is better than no father' persists, despite the large body of research that links violence against women to violence against children, and to a variety of post-traumatic stress disorders that develop in children who witness domestic violence.

The impact of domestic violence on children

In our study, children who had witnessed their mothers being physically assaulted displayed a variety of cognitive and behavioural disorders. An idealization of the father and the family continued to exist for some of the children amid great ambivalence and conflicted emotions, that ranged from denial to deep internal scars and an impaired sense of self and fragile identity. Lone's six-year-old son, Jesper, who witnessed the brutal battering of his mother, has many disturbed behaviour patterns, and after returning from his father was physically aggressive to his mother, saying, "You should have a knife in your back". A fragile child, he appeared fearful at the afterschool centre, and although his pedagogues describe him as a bright boy, he is failing at school – having difficulty concentrating and exhibiting multiple learning problems. Sanne's son, Kasper, who also witnessed his mother's assaults by his brother's father and was physically abused by his own father, is observed during a home visit and appears to be hyperactive, insecure, and has difficulty concentrating, although at the supportive environment of day care his pedagogue describes him as having made positive developmental progress. Gina's son, Jon, who witnessed the assault against his mother by his sister's father, has suffered multiple cognitive and behavioural disorders and is diagnosed as having attention deficit hyperactivity disorder (ADHD) – he is the child of generational family violence: a young battered mother who was also sexually abused as an adolescent, and a rejecting indifferent biological father. Carmina's three young children who also witnessed their mother being beaten were afraid to leave her for day care and have regressed developmentally. They were also afraid to visit their father who has physically abused them, and although they have been traumatized by the ongoing contact, their father is fighting for custody and may win. Zeinab's 10-year-old son has witnessed his mother being assaulted and has also been smashed against the wall by his father. As a young boy he was very afraid when his mother would leave him, and would exhibit great anxiety if she did not pick him up when expected at day care; now he occasionally expresses rage against his father. Emilie's two-year-old daughter has reacted to the trauma and violence by regressing and throwing many tantrums for hours and raging against Emilie. It is clear that many of these children who have witnessed family violence, and who themselves have been victims, have been deeply scarred by their experiences.

There is little doubt that witnessing violence damages children, and little attention has been paid to that phenomenon in family violence situations; nor to the fact that large numbers of children are endangered when their mothers are battered.

In the US, it is estimated that family violence is prevalent in three to four million homes and that over 3.3 million children witness violence every year. Children in violent homes face dual threats – the trauma of witnessing and being victims. Such children exhibit a variety of psycho-social and cognitive disorders: problems making friends, failing grades at school, school phobia, low self-esteem, sadness, depression, poor impulse control, and are at high risk for alcohol and drug abuse, isolation, loneliness and suicide (Jaffe et al, 1990). In a review of research regarding the impact of family violence on children's mental health, McCloskey et al (1995) point to increased anxieties, poor school performance, and conduct disorders including increased aggressiveness and impaired social problem-solving skills and high levels of psychopathology. Child witnesses and victims are now thought to be at risk for chronic trauma and post-traumatic stress disorders that emerge as deficits in school – particularly in the areas of cognitive and information processing skills – which result from dissociation, a common symptom of post-traumatic stress disorder (Fish-Murray, 1993; Rossman et al, 1994). Boys who have witnessed abuse are ten times more likely to batter their female partners as adults (US Senate Judiciary Committee, 1990), supporting the finding that violence is a learned behaviour (Walker, 1984). In battered women's childhoods, battering was reported in 67% of childhood homes (Walker, 1984), and 68% of abused wives had mothers who were similarly abused (Rosenbaum and O'Leary, 1981).

Studies of battered women indicate that a history of child sexual and physical abuse and witnessing the abuse of others in the home may predispose women to future victimization (National Clearinghouse for the Defense of Battered Women, 1994).

In Hester and Radford's study they found that children were assaulted as they attempted to protect their mothers from abuse, and of the 53 English mothers, 23 reported that their children had been physically and/or sexually abused by the fathers. They also reported that their children suffered from nightmares, emotional disturbances and speech disorders. In the Danish families 19 out of 26 women reported that their children had experienced combinations of psychological, physical and sexual abuse from the fathers, including a baby who was in the arms of its mother when assaulted, and children being beaten when they tried to protect their mothers (see also Christensen, 1988, 1999). Hester and Radford also found that violence against women was generally viewed as distinct and separate from child abuse by child welfare authorities and the courts (with the authorities in Denmark placing somewhat more emphasis than British authorities did on interventions in relation to children and displaying a slightly stronger awareness about children's safety).

However, in all countries discussed the general effects of family violence on children tended to be minimized by legal and social welfare authorities, although international research studies point to the severe impact of witnessing on children, the increased risks of physical abuse, as well as children's survival strategies (Christensen, 1988). And despite their large numbers, children who witness their mother's abuse remain a neglected constituency. Jurists rarely grapple with the plight of children who witness their mother's battering. "Although relevant to child custody decisions and child maltreatment allegations, child witnessing remains virtually hidden from decision rationales, policy initiatives, or even public debates" (Tomkins et al, 1994, pp 140-1).

Violent fathers' rights: contact and custody

Spousal [partner] abuse has a tremendous impact on children. Children learn several lessons in witnessing the abuse of one of their parents. First they learn that such behaviour appears to be approved by one of their most important role models and that violence toward a loved one is acceptable. Children also fail to grasp the full range of negative consequences for the violent behaviour and observe instead the short term reinforcements, namely compliance by the victim. Thus they learn the use of coercive power and violence as a way to influence loved ones ... in addition to the effect of the destructive modelling, children who grow up in violent homes experience damaging psychological effects.... (Chief Justice Workman, West Virginia Supreme Court, quoted in Tomkins et al, 1994)

In the United States, the landmark dissent of Chief Justice Workman of the West Virginia Supreme Court in a domestic violence custody case (*Patricia Ann S v James Daniel S [WV 1993]*) has set a legal precedent in terms of how courts consider male violence as a critical factor in custody decisions. Judge Workman argued that the damaging impact of witnessing family violence had been hitherto ignored by the courts and by child welfare authorities, and she recommended the retraining of court personnel and judiciary officials on the impact of domestic violence on children, and the risks posed to their physical and emotional safety. Fifteen states in the US have now passed legislation mandating that domestic violence should be considered a strong factor in custody and visitation decisions.

Clearly the impact of domestic violence on children raises questions about children's rights to a childhood free of violence, mothers' rights to human dignity and freedom from assault, and the rights of violent fathers to maintain control over their parenting relationships and parental authority. The ability of a violent father to adequately parent his child has not hitherto been focused on in Danish society. Many of the children in our study experienced neglect, abandonment, indifference, unpredictable behaviour, violence and drunkenness from their fathers; yet unsupervised visitation and in most cases, joint parental custody, was maintained. The women suffered bitter experiences and had no faith in the police, the courts, or the authorities to protect them or to gain redress and sole custody with control over the conditions of visitation.

As domestic violence creates such a central and destabilizing impact on mothers and children, with intergenerational time-bomb effects, it is vital to reconsider current Danish policies and practices that pertain to police protection, legal rights, visitation and custody agreements, and social welfare services, in order to support and protect – rather than further victimize – women who are battered by their partners. It is also imperative to rethink child welfare policies for children who are both witnesses and/or victims of family violence and who may experience undetected post-traumatic stress disorders.

SEVEN

Conclusion: Policy and practice recommendations

The lone mothers, whose stories of struggle and survival are told in this book, are neither exceptional nor unique. Rather their lives mirror the lives of many other low-income mothers in Denmark, where despite strong social insurance policies, families that are poor and female-headed are not faring well; and even more troubling, face decreasing social supports. The discourse of equality in Danish society serves to further stigmatize vulnerable lone mothers, who stand as living icons of 'failure' – because they appear not to have benefited from the well-praised public policies and practices designed to integrate them into civic and public life. They are perceived as 'problems' precisely because they failed to 'make it' within a universal society. However, it is clear that a large gap exists between universalism in theory and in practice, and that for vulnerable lone mothers the 'caring' obligations of the state are receding. Our study has uncovered many disturbing facets of welfare policies on-the-ground: a significant number of lone mothers and their children live on the outer periphery of equality facing economic hardships, social isolation and personal deprivations, experiences that stand in sharp contrast to the internal and international perceptions of the Danish welfare state.

The growing life disparities between those who are members of this new underclass and the rest of society is dramatic. Such inequality points to the urgent need to implement comprehensive structural changes with extended and targeted supports for marginalized groups. The findings of our qualitative study make visible the lives of those living in the shadows of universalism, and we hope that by shining a spotlight on the life-worlds of poor women and their children, we may inject an urgency and 'truth-telling' into the discourse about the social responsibilities of a welfare society and the impact of its social policies.

As we consider the major obstacles to family stability and independence emerging from our study, there are many spaces for intervention requiring vital changes at both local and national levels in order to build a more inclusive landscape of solidarity and collective responsibility (Jørgensen, 1999). In the sections that follow, key 'micro'-problem areas are summarized, followed by targeted interventions and recommendations which extend beyond to broader policy issues.

Social networks

Family networks were predominantly weak, absent, or characterized by insecurity and conflict. Frequently a conflicted family network shadowed a mother's whole life story, and many women related bitter stories about their own childhood experiences living with violence, alcohol, and parents in troubled marriages. Ongoing conflicts weighed heavily on several mothers in our group and for some led to a total break in contact with their parents. For others, such as ethnic minority lone mothers, geographic distance and custody restrictions separated them from their families of origin in their home countries. However, a few of the mothers in our study did experience close and helpful relationships with their children's grandparents, and these relationships were important at both a practical level and even more vital, at an emotional level. Babysitting, particularly when a child was ill, visiting and sharing experiences on weekends, and having an economic buffer were all identified as crucial forms of support. But such supportive family relationships were not the norm, and the majority of the lone mothers in our study described their family networks as sparse or non-existent.

Children's fathers

Contact with the children's fathers in almost all of the families in our study was problematic. Generally, the children's fathers were negative role models for their children: unstable, alcohol- or drug-abusing, violent, or had abandoned their children. Family violence, which created traumatic problems for both mothers and children, occurred in 11 of the 20 families. Even when violence was not part of the marriage or the household, children were treated callously by their fathers who did not maintain regular contact with them after separation.

Friends

Full-time parenting, lack of time, constant stress, isolation, and all-consuming children's needs left lone mothers little time to socialize, date, or make new friends. Lone mothers who lived in flats by themselves seemed to have minimal opportunities for frequent and supportive relations with other adults. For the mothers who were neither in the labour market nor in the educational system, there was little hope of building up supportive networks in either sphere. However, for those mothers who lived at Egmontgården, or in Boligfonden's communal house, social networks were formed that were mutually beneficial. These living spaces had an atmosphere of mutual tolerance, sensitivity and reciprocal support. When lone mothers moved away from these transitional settings, they experienced great difficulty finding similarly supportive networks.

The smallest network of mother and child

Several of the mothers expressed concerns about their strong attachments to their children. They pointed out the difficulties of loosening this tight liaison within a daily life where mother and child spent almost all free time alone together without grandparents, support from fathers, or social contacts with other adults and families (see Thams, 1999). A perpetually tight budget and, for some families, days with no money, seriously limited possibilities for an extended social life. Mothers were aware of the problems created for their children when daily living conditions isolated them from a broader social life. Bak's analysis of family networks in lone-parent families (Bak, 1997) indicated that lone mothers who succeeded in building 'extended family spaces' fared far better than those who remained isolated, and living in 'condensed family spaces' in which mother and child remained alone, leading to intense attachments and deep interdependence. Such intense and exclusive attachments between mothers and their children appeared closely related to the living conditions experienced by the mothers. Several studies (Fonagy et al, 1994) have identified stress, exhaustion and depression provoked by taxing living conditions as factors contributing to problematic attachments (fear of separation, for example) between mother and child. Children in our study also reacted differently to their mother's stress, were often insecure and demanding, lacking developmental autonomy, or their attachments to their mothers were manifested in hostile and aggressive behaviours. Some of the older children assumed the role of mother's confidante, assuming 'adultified' responsibilities. When family violence was involved, many children attempted to protect their mothers and were traumatized by witnessing assaults for which they often felt responsible. Few lone mothers in our study received constructive help to break unhealthy and isolated relationships with their children from either the social welfare or school systems. Where constructive help was received, it came from private agencies, pedagogues and health care professionals.

Professional networks

As we shift frames from inside the private family worlds of lone mothers and their children, to a broader focus on their communities and professional support networks, we briefly examine the roles of pedagogues in day care, teachers at school, and social workers at social welfare centres, private crisis centres, and other private organizations.

Day care

Day care played an enriching and supportive role in the lives of the children, and indirectly, in the lives of the lone mothers themselves. Nordic research has demonstrated that all children benefit more from attending day care than from staying at home, but this positive effect is clearest for children living in lone-parent families (Lassbo, 1988). For the children, day care became an important extension of the exclusive private sphere that they shared with their mothers (and in some cases, siblings), exposing them to a wider playful social world, expanding the circle of nurturing adults and enabling the children to form an independent peer social network. For children traumatized by family violence, the day care centre also functioned as an alternative life-world – a safe, free space with non-violent interactions which normalised daily life, and provided the possibility for therapeutic interventions.

Most of the mothers in our study expressed high levels of satisfaction about their children's day care experiences, from the structure and activities provided to the secure and trusting connections with day care pedagogues. Through this positive contact, mothers also received advice and counselling about how to handle difficulties with and concerns about their children, and appreciated the opportunity to share special moments and progress in their child's development. In a few situations in our study, the parent–pedagogue relationship was not handled with care and sensitivity, and in those cases lone mothers felt judged and stigmatized, their experiences mirroring other similarly negative treatment received at the hands of professionals at the social centres.

School

For those school-age children who had experienced domestic violence and unstable family lives with absent and alcoholic fathers, a wide array of emotional and cognitive impairments, including post-traumatic stress disorders, were present. Yet in most cases, comprehensive services were lacking, delayed, or non-existent, and many of the boys experienced neglect and indifference from teachers and school psychologists. During interviews with some of the teachers of the eight boys in the study, we became aware that many teachers knew very little about the complex and traumatic lives of the children: that a student had been witness to and victim of domestic violence, that a child with attention deficit hyperactivity disorder (ADHD) languished in school and was not seen for two years by a psychologist, that a young adolescent was under extreme stress when his brother's father was accused of sexually abusing a neighbour's daughter, that a young boy and his mother spent some period of time without a home. With one notable exception, where a lone mother described warm and supportive contacts at her son's small school, there was a vast divide between the home and school worlds of the children; the focus of school was on academics ignoring the multifaceted turbulent home lives that many of the children carried as heavy burdens daily to school. Consequently the most troubled children in our study spent many hours in their classrooms, either acting out or being extremely passive, with their learning disabilities and emotional impairments unattended to, receiving few remedial educational and psychological interventions. Like their mothers, their private lives were invisible, and they became lost boys in an indifferent school system.

Social centres

Throughout our study one theme dominated the mothers' narratives: humiliating and indifferent treatment at the social centres. Most mothers had extensive contacts with the social welfare system, and they bitterly described insensitive public social workers, disrespectful encounters and a lack of attention to their special needs. Apart from rare encounters with an exceptional social worker, the few positive encounters that did take place generally related to situations in which lone mothers were given extra financial subsidies to tide them over an acute crisis. The urgent concerns that they felt about their children's development were not often discussed during meetings with their social workers at the social centres, nor were their traumatic histories of domestic violence respected or addressed. The narrow interpretation of §43 and the refusal of many social workers to grant supportive services so that lone mothers could pursue an education was bitterly resented by the women whose applications were refused. Treatment also varied from one municipality to another so that local implementation of the *revalidering* provision placed the women in the role of beggars 'coming cap in hand' to the social centres as their rights to educational assistance were frequently denied.

Crisis centres and other private agencies

Several mothers, frustrated and at their wits' end from rejections and refusals at the social centres, sought out alternative sources of support through their contacts with private agencies such as Boligfonden and other private crisis centres. It became apparent during the course of extended interviews with the mothers that their experiences with social workers at private agencies were usually positive and that these social workers provided a lifeline in times of acute need. Although private agencies could not provide ongoing economic support to the mothers, they played a vital role in advocating for their clients and pressuring the social centres (and even angry creditors) to provide more assistance. The mothers described both the private social workers and the agencies in glowing terms: as one "who listens, who always believes what I am telling him and he never moralizes", of crisis centres without which they "could not have survived". These images of social workers as empathic, reliable, supportive professionals stood in sharp contrast to the descriptions by lone mothers of their experiences in the social centres, women to be heard, to talk about multiple problems and burdens and to voice concerns about their children. Rather they felt controlled, under surveillance and alienated by a large bureaucracy with inflexible standards (see Halskov, 1999, 2000).

Health and vulnerability

Sick children

More than half the mothers in our study struggled to cope with sick children which severely constrained their own opportunities in terms of education, training and the labour market. In some cases where social networks were frayed or non-existent, they themselves became ill from stress, had to drop out or postpone education, or lost their jobs. In other cases, complicated and inappropriate care arrangements were made which necessitated an older child staying home from school to take care of a younger sick sibling.

The frequent illnesses that the children suffered imposed ongoing burdens on their mothers: ear infections (several drains set up, resistance to antibiotic medications, impaired hearing); bed wetting; asthma and bronchial ailments; damage to teeth because of the side-effects of medications; diffuse stomach pains; eating disorders; repeated hernia operations; and ADHD. Very much alone in their concern and anxiety for their sick children, the lone mothers also had to cope with an almost endless round of visits to hospitals, doctors and pharmacies, necessitating additional expenses for certain medications, transport to doctors, and further visits to the social centres trying to secure extra economic assistance for their children's health needs.

The relationship between the quality of housing and children's health has long been documented in Danish research (Christensen, 1956; Andersen, 1981). Andersen's longitudinal social medicine study across three decades demonstrated the devastating impact of social strains and pressures, including bad housing conditions, on children in later years. Disturbing accounts about unfit housing conditions emerged time and again from the mothers' narratives in our study: no bath, no hot water, inadequate heating, dangerous gas stoves, cold, dampness – all of which played a role in exacerbating children's health problems. Recommendations from doctors that mothers be given better flats were routinely ignored by the social centres, and it took persistence, confrontation and innovative scheming by the mothers, and often advocacy interventions on the part of private agencies, to secure decent flats which usually resulted in improved health for their families.

It was clear that children's illnesses played a major role in determining a mother's ability to enter and/or remain in the labour market or to pursue an education, and the lack of available sick days that employees were entitled to take for sick children proved another key impediment. In contrast to Sweden's generous sick child leave where parents may stay home with a sick child during an illness, Danish parents are generally permitted to take leave only on the first day of their child's illness without loss of pay (and many parents use the 'first day' leave several times); but with frequently sick children and no back-up child care arrangements, many lone mothers faced limited employment prospects and often experienced labour market discrimination, as they were not viewed as reliable employees.

Sick mothers

Not only did the children in our study suffer from high rates of illness, but their mothers' health was compromised as well. We noted many psychological problems – paralysing anxiety, depression, post-traumatic stress disorders, and a range of physical symptoms that appeared to be stress-relaed: exhaustion, migraine headaches, muscle tension, dizziness and fainting. In their narratives, the mothers constantly referred to the many pressures they experienced and subsequent somatized symptoms. Very little research to date has been conducted about lone mothers' health in Denmark, but in Sweden, the Folkhälsoinstituttet's analysis (1994) points to both a lack of protective factors and a lack of feelings of coherence about one's life as the central causes of poor health. Antonovsky's earlier (1987) study supported this finding, arguing that health problems improve when life becomes coherent and manageable. Lacking both protective factors and a sense of coherence and control over their lives and that of their children, lone mothers became even more vulnerable when confronted by a loss of health, and overwhelmed by anxiety about ongoing illness.

Stigmatization

The lack of a supportive network of friends and family, the indifferent treatment by social workers at the social centres, the problems of illness affecting both lone mothers and their children – all served to create a sense of vulnerability and impaired self-esteem, heightened by stigmatizing public perceptions about their lone mother status. Many complained bitterly about being strung along for months or years by the social system, humiliated by uncaring and indifferent treatment, made to feel "like an idiot", frustrated by the many denials of §43 and offers of only low-level training. Other lone mothers in our study reported feeling targeted and discriminated against in their daily lives, describing encounters which reeked of prejudice: mothers from Egmontgården (well-known throughout the city of Copenhagen as a lone-mother facility) experienced problems buying TV sets on installment plans once their address was known; others reported that they had difficulty obtaining telephones and were required to pay three months in advance for services.

Being a low-income lone mother, unemployed, and dependent on the social system, created a sense of marginalization which was exacerbated if the women had experienced family violence, or if they were immigrants. As we noted in Chapter 6, discrimination by the police and judicial system particularly afflicted those lone mothers whose lives were further stigmatized by family violence. Many women who were survivors of family violence also experienced shame and humiliation about the violence and felt negatively judged by family and neighbours, thereby increasing their own sense of marginalization.

*   *   *   *

Policy and practice recommendations

A three-year detailed look inside the lives of lone mothers and their children has revealed grave disparities between what is and what ought to be – between a secure, stable and comfortable world that most Danes reside in, and a shadow world in which fear, insecurity and diminished rights are pervasive. We share the view that social policies must respond to the needs and life-worlds of marginalized social groups, and it is clear that the experiences of the lone mothers and their children in our study do not correspond with socially responsible welfare policies. Rather, our study has uncovered stressed and often desperate family worlds – mothers and children living compromised and diminished lives in which they are confronted by a multitude of social strains, although they live in a prosperous country with internationally admired and respected social policies. It is our hope that their individual life stories may provide a framework for understanding the unique difficulties that they face, and lead to the development of policies that address the critical problems of economically and socially vulnerable lone mothers and their children. Their dramatic life stories demand a rethinking of the principles undergirding the rapidly transforming economic and social foundations of the Danish state – a welfare society at the crossroads (Reintoft, 1998). Hence we propose both policy and practice recommendations grounded in the existential realities of the families in our study.

Our objectives in formulating these proposals are to promote a different public discourse about lone mothers in need, and to reshape policies that create substantial and beneficial changes in their lives. We argue for the promotion of social practices that offer opportunity and empowerment without accompanying condescension and humiliation towards beneficiaries. Such practices combine an in-depth knowledge of vulnerable lone-mother families, a readiness to offer opportunities that empower and are oriented to serving their best interests and those of their children, and a belief in their potential to cope with the difficult and complex situations in their own lives. Sincerity and openness should be the cornerstone for genuine help and cooperation based on three guiding principles: comprehensiveness, respect for the individual's aspirations and social integration. This perspective is foundational to both the social policy changes and the interventions we propose.

- Comprehensiveness: a comprehensive approach is always directed towards both mother and children. The whole family is not only considered a basic foundation in the lives of these women, but the family is also understood as the fundamental meaning of their lives and the reason for their struggles. Comprehensiveness demands close cooperation between the different intervening agencies operating in the life space of the family and is based on a cross-disciplinary way of thinking and acting, an agreement on integrated general principles, and an openness and readiness to revise the approach in dialogue with the mother, with a focus on long-term sustainable gains rather than on cheap quick-fix solutions.
- Respecting individual aspirations: practising respect means respecting the goals and aspirations of a lone mother, believing in her capacity to take care of herself, even if, from the point of view

of the social system, she may not have made the wisest decisions. Such an approach is non-judgmental and includes respect for the struggles of the mother, for her life situation and recognition of her resilience.

- Social integration: vulnerable lone mothers must be seen as valued members of a social community. Social support measures, designed to strengthen social and community integration, must be flexible, providing and restoring resources and building competence and 'social capital' as part of long-term family stability. Cultural differences must be respected and discrimination against ethnic minority women confronted and their rights protected, so that social integration is promoted for all members of the society.

Towards a reformulation of social policy and practice

By the term 'social policy' we refer not only to legal regulations as they are defined in parliamentary Acts and implemented in social welfare laws, but we also include other fields of practice, such as housing, education, the administration of justice, including the police force, as well as municipalities, social welfare centres, private and community agencies, day care institutions and schools. In other words, by 'social policy' we refer to the totality of legal provisions, social benefits, supports and interventions, which should be changed so that lone-mother families may find an equal and full place at the Danish table. Our recommendations cover six broad areas: education, housing, domestic violence, schools and day care centres, legal rights and networks.

Education

Education is the path out of poverty to a sustainable family future, enabling lone mothers to earn adequate incomes and become economically self-sufficient. Education should be seen as a long-term family investment, and all occupations should be seen as open opportunities for lone mothers as opposed to gendered low-level training. Educational support through §43 *revalidering* should be available to all lone mothers who demonstrate educational aspirations and a commitment to post-secondary education or vocational training.

- Previous experiences, qualifications and aspirations should be integrated in the course of planning educational programmes; and education and training that leads to economic independence in viable occupational or professional employment through well-paying jobs should be promoted.

- The practical realities of a low-income household absorbing extra child care costs, transport costs, as well as other stressful family dynamics must be addressed, and resources made available to enable mothers to succeed in their programmes of study. Special support services, including the care of sick children, as well as child care subsidies for evening and odd-hours care should be made available to lone mothers.
- The option of enrolling in training courses at the so-called AMU-centres (Labour Market Educational Centres) should be permitted for lone mothers (and all persons on welfare allowances) who are not members of a union.
- Work activation policies (a mandatory work requirement which must be accepted to secure a welfare subsidy) should not be imposed on lone mothers and should never be required at the cost of social integration or when comprehensive support services are not available.

Housing

Acute housing needs keep many lone-mother families in social misery. In the absence of explicit housing provisions for lone mothers, they are dependent on limited availability of social housing and the expensive private market. While income-based housing subsidies are available to all renters, the increasingly privatized housing market has resulted in less affordable housing, and low-income lone mothers frequently end up living in unhealthy flats in strained surroundings isolated from social networks. Therefore housing policies must be changed to explicitly address the needs of vulnerable groups, such as lone mothers and their children.

- A quota of flats should be reserved in every municipality for low-income lone-parent families and active support should be provided for each family in its efforts to secure decent flats at affordable rents.
- Housing subsidies should be increased to reflect the current market rates of housing in Copenhagen as well as other urban and rural areas.
- Housing collectives for lone mothers and their children should be established with on-site facilities, such as day care and social

workers, thereby providing ready access to both social and professional networks.

Domestic violence

Domestic violence emerged as an all-too pervasive experience in the lives of many lone mothers in our study and continues to exist in a culture of silence. There is public silence and minimal legislative action about this critical violation of women's rights, maintained by the private shame and the hidden injuries of victims and survivors. The emotional devastation and destabilized family worlds caused by such violence must become part of a new public discourse that focuses on all women's rights to protection of their personhood from intimate partner violence. The damaging impact on children who have been witness to, and victims of, domestic violence is, as yet, untold: post-traumatic stress disorders, social and cognitive impairments and physical illnesses. Mothers and children assaulted by domestic violence must be offered therapeutic interventions. The interventions should:

- Focus on changing the culture of denial about family violence to a culture of visibility and recognize that domestic violence is neither a 'communication' nor an 'interpersonal dynamics' problem, but rather a crime deeply embedded in patriarchal power. All front-line professionals – psychologists, social workers, teachers, pedagogues, and police – should be informed and educated about the pervasiveness of the problem and the severe social and psychological consequences for mothers and their children.
- Establish a comprehensive response system between police agencies and support structures in the social system, so that victims of violence are offered physical protection as well as emotional and practical assistance in a speedy and efficient manner.

Support for children who have experienced domestic violence should focus on developing integrated services between the child's school or day care centre, crisis centre, social centre and police authorities. Both schools and day care centres are positioned to play a crucial role in the child's development and recovery from trauma. Stability of routines in a safe environment and the opportunity to develop close attachments to caring and sensitive adult professionals are vital. We propose that:

- Schools and day care centres develop explicitly formulated policies towards family violence with clear obligations to report to the police any knowledge of such incidents.
- Such policies must be oriented towards a strategy of prevention, including detection of symptoms at an early stage and access to relevant social and psychological interventions, to ensure that therapeutic treatment is always available for children who demonstrate behavioural cues about exposure to violence.
- Schools and day care centres ensure that teachers and school staff are given training about the nature and causes of post-traumatic stress disorder syndrome so that they recognize behavioural symptoms and respond in appropriate and developmentally supportive ways; and that this training includes an understanding of obstacles to learning caused by children's traumatic social and emotional experiences.
- Schools and day care centres foster close cooperation and trust among mother, child, the social welfare system and school and day care authorities.
- Schools emphasize the importance of creating a supportive social climate in the classroom and fostering non-violent relationships among children.
- The municipalities ensure that young children exposed to violence receive priority placement in day care centres, and that special treatment programmes are in place at day care centres to handle the emotional damage and trauma internalized by very young children.

Family violence and legal rights

Many women have experienced terror and brutality at the hands of their male partners yet have been accorded few protections and rights by the police and legal authorities. The emphasis of child welfare authorities and the courts on maintaining child contact with a violent father places women at grave personal risk and should be revisited. Danish laws and practices that pertain to police protection, injunctions, visitation and custody should be radically revised in order to support and protect, rather than further victimize, mothers who are battered by their children's fathers. Children's rights to a childhood free from violence should be emphasized with the recognition that children's 'best interests' are not served when violent fathers maintain free access to and control over mothers and children. In order to redress the continuing injustices of domestic violence, speedy reforms need to be implemented in the following areas:

- The judicial system must confront domestic violence as a crime so that women's and children's rights to a life free from violence are enforced, and violent assaults against family members are severely punished. Mothers should have easy access to obtaining injunctions (*Tilhold*), irrespective of the custody status of the children, and police officers must both enforce injunctions and arrest perpetrators of violence in accordance with the penal code §265.
- Judicial hearings to determine custody and visitation for children in families where domestic assaults have occurred should take place in a secure family court with police protection available to the mother; the proceedings should include child hearings which rely on the expertise of professional child psychologists and educators.
- Joint custody of children should not be granted in families where domestic violence has occurred, and an evaluation of parental fitness should always include reports of past family violence and an assessment of current safety needs of mother and children.
- Children should be respected in their rights to refuse visitation with violent fathers, and if visitation takes place it should occur in supervised public settings.
- Immigrant women who are disadvantaged by their foreign status should receive specialized legal services to maintain their custody rights in custody disputes with Danish husbands, and culturally sensitive social services should be available to help cope with the trauma of domestic violence.

Social and professional networks

In order to strengthen families disempowered by ongoing stress, isolation and family violence, social integration must be promoted at all levels, both formal and informal.

Professional networks, specifically social welfare centres, need to undergo an institutional self-evaluation in order to radically reform the culture of humiliation that appears pervasive in the public agencies. Policies and practices that undermine lone mothers and perpetuate their vulnerable status must be examined and changed. Much can be learned from the comprehensive advocacy work of professionals in private agencies. Fostering social networks in the communities and

and municipalities in which lone mothers live will further strengthen possibilities of social integration and the following measures are recommended:

- Establish social support groups based in health care or day care institutions so that vulnerable lone mothers can share their experiences in a therapeutic setting.
- Establish lone-mother self-help groups within the municipalities.
- Ensure additional resources are made available in the social system in order to strengthen the social networks of vulnerable families.
- Establish social support and advocacy groups for immigrant women.

Concluding reflections

We are fully aware that our recommendations do not point towards quick and easy solutions for vulnerable lone-mother families, that, at present, the social system places more obstacles than supports in their paths, leading many lone mothers to feel a deep sense of injustice about the way they are devalued in Danish society. We believe that all solutions – from the micro-level of one individual's daily life to the broader national policy level – must be informed and shaped by the existential realities on the ground: at each social centre, each municipality, each school, each day care centre. And we believe there is much to learn by listening to the voices of those who, hitherto, have been unheard and invisible. As researchers and advocates – two Danes and one American – embodying both insider and outsider cultural perspectives, we have forcefully realized that the social democratic values of the welfare state, the focus on equality, and the universalistic welfare policies originally designed to treat lone mothers as equal citizens no longer extend their reach to all.

Discrimination in labour markets, restricted opportunities for post-secondary education, lack of legal protections against family violence, poor housing conditions, narrowed social networks, isolation, ethnic discrimination, poverty of time and material resources, including care provisions for sick children and public stigmatization – parallel increased cuts in the Danish welfare state over the past four years, and policy shifts favouring 'work activation' and 'personal responsibility' with a decreasing emphasis on social citizenship rights and entitlements. This postmodern 'market' view of lone motherhood ominously points to a gradual erosion of rights which have taken place so rapidly elsewhere in the US and

Britain. The consequences for children are devastating: unhappy and damaged childhoods and social and cognitive impairments.

For lone mothers and their children who live on the outer boundaries of universalism, the slow erosion of their rights remain largely invisible, masked by the overarching mantle of equality. The recognition and confrontation of this growing challenge to the equality dilemma – the diminished rights of lone mothers and their children – will clearly prove a litmus test for Denmark's social democracy in the coming millennium.

References

Abraham, L. (1993) *Mama might be better off dead: The failure of health care in America*, Chicago, IL: University of Chicago Press.

Alsted Research (1998) *Undersøgelse af fattigdommen i Danmark [Study on poverty in Denmark]*, Udført for dagbladet, *Aktuelt*, København: Trykt I Focus Efterår.

Amaro, H., Fried, L., Cabral, H. and Zuckerman, B. (1990) 'Violence during pregnancy and substance use', *American Journal of Public Health*, vol 80, no 5, pp 575-9.

Andersen, T.F. (1981) *Børns opvækstvilkår i langsigtet perspektiv – en socialmedicinsk forløbsundersøgelse gennem tre artier [Children growing up in a long-range perspective – a social medicine follow-up study through three decades]*, København: Rapport 23 (Copenhagen, report no 23, Institute for Social Medicine).

Antonovsky, A. (1987) *Unraveling the mystery of health: How people manage stress and stay well*, San Francisco, CA: Jossey-Bass.

Bak, M. (1997) *Enemorfamilien [The lone mother family]*, København: Forlaget Sociologi.

Bassuk, E.L. (1990) 'Who are the homeless families? Characteristics of sheltered mothers and children', *Community Mental Health Journal*, vol 26, no 5, pp 425-34.

Bassuk, E.L., Weinreb, L.F., Buckner, J.C., Browne, A., Salomon, A. and Bassuk, S.S. (1996) 'The characteristics and needs of sheltered homeless and low-income housed mothers', *Journal of the American Medical Association*, vol 276, no 8, pp 640-6.

Björnberg, U. (1997) 'Single mothers in Sweden: supported workers who mother', in S. Duncan and R. Edwards (eds) *Single mothers in an international context*, London: UCL Press, pp 241-68.

Bohn, D. (1990) 'Domestic violence and pregnancy: implications for practice', *Journal of Nurse-Midwifery*, vol 35, no 2, pp 86-98.

Bradshaw, J. and Millar J. (1991) *Lone parent families in the UK*, London: HMSO.

Bronfenbrenner, U. (1995) *Examining lives in context: Perspectives on the ecology of human development*, Washington, DC: American Psychological Association.

Campbell, J. (1986) 'Nursing assessment for risk of homicide with battered women', *Advances in Nursing Science*, vol 8, no 4, July, pp 36-51.

Children's Defense Fund (1996) *The state of America's children: Yearbook*, Washington, DC: Author.

Children's Defense Fund (1998) *The state of America's children: Yearbook*, Washington, DC: Author.

Children's Defense Fund (1999) *The state of America's children: Yearbook*, Washington, DC: Author.

Children's Defense Fund (2000) *The state of America's children: Yearbook*, Washington, DC: Author.

Christensen, E. (1988) *Opvækst eller overlevelse. Psykisk forsvar mod vold og strategier for overlevelse hos 4-6-årige børn i familier med hustrumishandling* [*Growing up or surviving. Psychic defense against violence and strategies for survival among 4-6 year old children in families with violence against the mother*], København: Sikon.

Christensen, E. (1999) 'Social arv i familier med vold mod mor' [*Social heritage in families with violence against the mother*], *Social Forskning*, Temanummer, December, pp 88-97.

Christensen, V. (1956) *Boligforhold og børnesygelighed* [*Housing conditions and child morbidity*], København: Munksgård.

Coles, R. and Coles, J.H. (1989) *Women of crisis: Lives of struggle and hope*, Reading, MA: Addison Wesley.

Cooper, Y. (1996) 'Me Blair, you Clinton', *New Statesman*, 9 August, pp 10-11.

Danish Board for Ethnic Equality (October 2000) *Denmark's fourth periodic report concerning the International Covenant on Civil and Political Rights*, Copenhagen: Author.

Danmarks Statistik (Danish Statistical Bureau) (1994) Compiled by Bodil Stensvig, Copenhagen.

Denzin, N.M. and Lincoln, Y. (eds) (1998) *Collecting and interpreting qualitative materials*, Thousand Oaks, CA: Sage Publications.

DeParle, J. (1994) 'Momentum builds for cutting back welfare system', *The New York Times*, 13 November, p 1.

Dominelli, L. (1988) *Anti-racist social work: A challenge for white educators*, London: Macmillan.

Dominelli, L. (1997) *Anti-racist social work* (2nd edn), London: Macmillan.

DSS (Department of Social Security) (1998) *A new contract for welfare*, Cm 3805, London: The Stationery Office.

Duncan, S. and Edwards, R. (1997a) 'Single mothers in Britain: unsupported workers or mothers?', in S. Duncan and R. Edwards (eds) *Single mothers in an international context: Mothers or workers?*, London: UCL Press, pp 45-79.

Duncan, S. and Edwards, R. (eds) (1997b) *Single mothers in an international context: Mothers or workers?*, London: UCL Press.

Duncan, S. and Edwards, R. (1999) *Lone mothers, paid work and gendered moral rationalities*, London: Macmillan.

Ebb, N. (1994) *Child care tradeoffs: States make painful choices*, Washington, DC: Children's Defense Fund.

Edelson, J. (1995) *Violence against women research workshop*, Washington, DC: National Institute of Justice.

Edwards, J. and Mckie, L. (1993/94) 'The European Economic Community: a vehicle for promoting equal opportunities in Britain', *Critical Social Policy*, vol 13, no 3, pp 51-65.

Egelund, T. and Halskov, T. (1990) *Udvikling af det sociale arbejde* [*Development of social work*], København: Munksgård.

Ehrenreich, B. and Piven, F.F. (1984) 'The feminization of poverty; when the family wage system breaks down', *Dissent*, vol 31, Spring, pp 162-70.

Ejrnæs, M. (1999) 'En regering og et folketing, der er mere fremmedfjendsk end befolkningen' ['A government and parliament being more xenophobic than ordinary people'], *Social Politik*, no 2, pp 2-10.

Esping-Andersen, G. (1990) *The three worlds of welfare capitalism*, Cambridge: Polity Press.

EUROSTAT (1997) *Income distribution*, Brussels: EU Commission, May.

Fekete, L. (1997) 'Blackening the economy: the path to convergence', *Race and Class*, vol 39, no 2, pp 1-17.

Fekete, L. (1998/99) 'Popular racism in corporate Europe', *Race and Class*, vol 40, no 2/3, pp 1-17.

Fish-Murray, C. (1993) 'Childhood trauma and subsequent suicidal behavior', in A.A. Leenaars (ed) *Suicidology*, Northvale, NJ: Jason Aronson, pp 73-92.

Folkhälsoinstituttet (1994) *Ensamma mammor. En rapport om ensamstående mödrars hälsa och livsvillkor* [*Lone mothers. A report on health and living conditions of lone mothers*], Stockholm: Folkhälsoinstituttet, no 24.

Fonagy, P., Steele, M., Steele, H., Higgit A. and Target, M. (1994) 'Emanuel Millar Memorial Lecture 1992: the theory and practice of resilience', *Journal of Child Psychology and Psychiatry and Allied Disciplines*, vol 35, no 2, pp 231-57.

Ford, J., Rompf, E., Faragher, T. and Weisenfluh, S. (1995) 'Case outcomes in domestic violence court: influence of judges', *Psychological Reports*, vol 77, no 2, pp 587-94.

Geertz, C. (1973) *The interpretations of cultures: Selected essays*, New York, NY: Basic Books.

Goldberg, G.S. and Kremen, E. (1990) *The feminization of poverty: Only in America?*, New York, NY: Greenwood Press.

Gordon, L. (ed) (1990) *Women, the state and welfare*, Madison, WI: University of Wisconsin Press.

Guttenplan, D. and Margaronis, M. (26 June 2000) 'Letter from London', *The Nation*, vol 270, no 25, pp 23-6.

Habermas, J. (1971) *Knowledge and human interests*, Boston, MA: Beacon Press.

Halskov, T. (1994) *Liden tue kan vælte stort læs: om enlige mødre i EU. Tre eksempler: Tyskland, Italien, Danmark* [*Little stroke fell great oaks: On lone mothers in the EU. Three examples: Germany, Italy and Denmark*], Copenhagen: Socialpolitisk Forening og Forlag.

Halskov, T. (1999) 'Trængte eneforsørgerfamilier' ['Lone mothers in need'], in L. Dencik and P. Schultz Jørgensen (eds) *Børn og familie i det postmoderne samfund* [*Children and family in post-modern society*], København: Hans Reitzels Forlag, pp 461-76.

Halskov, T. (2000) 'Enlige mødre i Danmark og Sverige. Mellem offentlig og privat velfærd' ['Lone mothers in Denmark and Sweden. Between public and private welfare'], *Social Vetenskapeligt Tidskrift*, vol 7, no 1-2, pp 72-86.

Hansen, E. and Østvand, A. (1998) *Med forlov. En undersøgelse af politiets praksis i hustruvoldsager* [*A study on police practice in cases with domestic violence*], Copenhagen (unpublished).

Hansen, E.J. (1986) *Danskernes levekår: 1986 sammenholdt med 1976* [*Living conditions of the Danes: 1986 compared to 1976*], København: Hans Reitzels Forlag.

Hansen, E.J. (1989) *Fattigdom* [*Poverty*], København: Socialforskningsinstituttet, no 89, p 5.

Helburn, S. (ed) (1995) *Cost, quality and child outcomes in child care centers*, University of Colorado at Denver (ERIC Document Reproduction Service, no ED 386 297).

Herbert, T., Silver, R. and Ellard, J. (1991) 'Coping with an abusive relationship: how and why do women stay', *Journal of Marriage and the Family*, vol 53, May, pp 311-25.

Hernes, H. (1987) *Welfare state and woman power: Essays in state feminism*, Oslo: Scandinavian University Press.

Hester, M. and Radford, L. (1996) *Domestic violence and child contact arrangements in England and Denmark*, Bristol/York: The Policy Press/ Joseph Rowntree Foundation.

Hetherington, E.M. (ed) (1999) *Coping with divorce, single parenting, and remarriage: A risk and resiliency perspective*, Mahwah, NJ: Lawrence Erlbaum Associates.

Hobson, B. (1994) 'Solo mothers, social policy regimes and the logics of gender', in D. Sainsbury (ed) *Gendering welfare states*, London: Sage Publications, pp 170-87.

Hotaling, G. and Sugarman, D. (1986) 'An analysis of risk markers in husband to wife violence: the current state of knowledge', *Violence and Victims*, vol 1, no 2, Summer, pp 101-24.

Hurstel, F. (1993) 'The social role and psychological function of the father in the family of today', in *Fathers in families of tomorrow*, Copenhagen: Ministry of Social Affairs, pp 179-92.

Ingerslev, O., Ploug, N. and Reib, J. (1992) *Forløbsanalyser af de 25-29-årige i 1980'erne* [*Rolling survey of the 25-59 year old persons during the 1980s*], København: Socialkommissions sekretariat.

Jaffe, P., Wolfe, A. and Wilson, S. (1990) *Children of battered women*, Newbury Park, CA: Sage Publications.

Jain, R. (1997) 'Fortifying the fortress: immigration and policies in the European Union', *International Studies*, vol 34, no 2, pp 163-80.

Jalmert, L. (1993) 'The father's role in the child's development', in *Fathers in families of tomorrow*, Copenhagen: Ministry of Social Affairs, pp 76-106.

Jeppesen, K.J. (1995) *Ethnic minorities in Denmark*, Copenhagen: Danish National Institute of Social Research.

Jones, A. (1991) *Women who kill*, London: Victor Gollancz.

Jørgensen, P.S. (1999) 'Barnet i risikofamilien' ['The child in the at-risk family'], in L. Dencik and P.S. Jørgensen (eds) *Børn og familie i det postmoderne samfund* [*Children and family in the post-modern family*], København: Hans Reitzels Forlag, pp 403-21.

Kahn, P. and Polakow, V. (2000) 'Mothering denied: commodification and caregiving under new US welfare laws', *Sage Race Relations Abstracts*, vol 25, no 1, pp 7-25.

Kamerman, S.G. and Kahn, A.J. (eds) (1991) *Child care, parental leave, and the under 3's: Policy innovation in Europe*, New York, NY: Auburn House.

Kamerman, S.G. and Kahn, A.J. (1995) *Starting right: How America neglects its youngest children and what we can do about it*, New York, NY: Oxford University Press.

Lamb, M. (ed) (1986) *The father's role: Applied perspectives*, Chichester: Wiley.

Larsen, J.E. and Sørensen, A.M. (1994) 'Lone parents', in S. Carlsen and J.L. Larsen (eds) *The equality dilemma*, Copenhagen: The Danish Equal Status Council, pp 143-53.

Lassbo, G. (1988) *Mamma – (pappa) – barn [Mum – (dad) – child]*, Dissertation, Göteborg Studies in Educational Sciences, no 68, Gothenburg, Sweden: Gothenburg University.

Lewis, J. (ed) (1997) *Lone mothers in European welfare regimes: Shifting policy logics*, London: Jessica Kingsley Publishers.

Lewis, L. (1998) '"Work", "welfare", and lone mothers', *The Political Quarterly*, vol 69, no 1, pp 4-13.

Lister, R. (1994) 'The Child Support Act: shifting family obligations in the United Kingdom', *Social Politics*, vol 1, no 2, Summer, pp 211-22.

McCloskey, L., Figueredo, A. and Koss, M. (1995) 'The effects of systemic family violence on children's mental health', *Child development*, vol 66, no 5, October, pp 1239-61.

McClure, B. (1996) 'Domestic violence: the role of the health care professional', *Michigan Family Review*, vol 2, no 1, pp 63-75.

Mink, G. (1998) *Welfare's end*, Ithaca, NY: Cornell University Press.

Mirrlees-Black, C. (1995) 'Estimating the extent of domestic violence: findings from the BCS', *Research Bulletin*, no 37, Home Office Research and Statistics Department, London: Whiting and Birch.

Murray, C. (1993) 'The coming white underclass', *Wall Street Journal*, 29 October, p A14.

National Clearinghouse on Family Violence (1991) *Wife abuse: The impact on children*, Ottowa: Author, February.

National Clearinghouse for the Defense of Battered Women (1994), *Statistics packet* (3rd edn), Philadelphia, PA: Author.

National Coalition for the Homeless (1996) *Welfare repeal: Moving Americans off welfare into homelessness*, Washington, DC: Author.

'New Deal for Lone Parents: Statistics' (3 February 2000) www.dfee.gov.uk

Pearce, D. (1978) 'The feminization of poverty: women, work and welfare', *The Urban and Social Change Review*, vol 11, nos 1-2, pp 28-36.

Pedersen, P. and Smith, N. (1999) 'Undersøgelse af lavindkomstgrupper', Centeret for arbejdsmarkeds – og sociale analyzer ['Study of low-income groups', Center for Labor Market Studies and Social Policy Analysis], Århus University (cited in Aktuelt 16 March 1999).

Piven, F.P. (1995) 'Foreword', in S. Schram, *Words of welfare: The poverty of social science and the social science of poverty*, Minneapolis: University of Minnesota Press, pp ix-xv.

Polakow, V. (1993) *Lives on the edge: Single mothers and their children in the other America*, Chicago, IL: Univeristy of Chicago Press.

Polakow, V. (1996) 'Chronic poverty and the struggle for family survival. The rhetoric and reality of welfare reform', *Michigan Family Review*, vol 2, no 2, pp 25-39.

Polakow, V. (1997) 'The shredded net: the end of welfare as we knew it', *Sage Race Relations Abstracts*, vol 22, no 3, pp 3-22.

Proceedings of the House of Commons Employment Committee (1995) *Mothers in employment*, vol 1, London: HMSO, HC-227-1, 15 February.

Reintoft, H. (1998) *Træd varsomt: Dansk socialpolitik ved en skillevej* [*Walk carefully: Danish social policy at a crossroad*], København: Hans Reitzels Forlag.

Roll, J. (1992) *Lone parents in the European community*, London: European Family and Policy Unit.

Rosenbaum, A. and O'Leary, D. (1981) 'Children: the unintended victims of marital violence', *American Journal of Orthopsychiatry*, vol 51, no 4, pp 692-9.

Roseneil, S. and Mann, K. (1996) 'Unpalatable choices and inadequate families: lone mothers and the underclass debate', in E.B. Silva (ed) *Good enough mothering? Feminist perspectives on lone motherhood*, London: Routledge, pp 191-210.

Ross, H. and Sawhill, I. (1975) *Time of transition: The growth of families headed by women*, Washington, DC: Urban Institute.

Rossman, B.B., Mallah, K., Dominguez, M., Kimura, S. and Boyer-Sneed, G. (1994) 'Cognitive and social information processing of children in violent families', Paper presented at the *American Psychological Association*, Los Angeles (ERIC Document Reproduction Service, no ED 379 540).

Scheffer-Kumpula, M. (2000) 'Om en utsatt kategori kvinnor' ['About a vulnerable group of women'], *Socialvetenskaplig Tidskrift*, vol 7, nos 1-2, pp 87-108.

Scheper-Hughes, N. (1992) *Death without weeping: The violence of everyday life in Brazil*, Berkeley, CA: University of California Press.

Schram, S. (1995) *Words of welfare: The poverty of social science and the social science of poverty*, Minneapolis: University of Minnesota Press.

Shepard, M. (1992) 'Child-visiting and domestic abuse,' *Child Welfare*, vol 71, no 4, July-August, pp 357-67.

Sherman, A., Armey, C., Duffield, B., Ebb, N. and Weinstein, D. (1998) *Welfare to what? Early findings on family hardship and well-being*, Washington, DC: Children's Defense Fund and National Coalition for the Homeless.

Siim, B. (1997) 'Dilemmas of citizenship in Denmark: lone mothers between work and care', in J. Lewis (ed) *Lone mothers in European welfare regimes: Shifting policy logics*, London: Jessica Kingsley Publishers, pp 140-70.

Sinfield, A. (1994) 'The latest trends in social security in the United Kingdom', in N. Ploug and J. Kvist (eds) *Recent trends in cash benefits in Europe*, Copenhagen: The Danish National Institute of Social Research, pp 123-47.

Skytte, M. (1997) *Etniske minoritetsfamilier og socialt arbejde* [*Ethnic minority families and social work*], København: Hans Reitzel Forlag.

Smith, N. and Naur, M. (1998) 'Cohort effects on the gender wage gap', in I. Persson and C. Jonung (eds) *Women's work wages*, London: Routledge.

Socialministeriet (1998) *Vejledning om lov om aktiv socialpolitik* [*Order on act of active social policy*], Socialministeriets vejledning af 5 Marts.

Stack, C. (1974) *All our kin: Strategies for survival in a black community*, New York, NY: Harper & Row.

Stack, C. (1996) *Call to home: African Americans reclaim the rural south*, New York, NY: Beacon.

Steinbock, M. (1995) 'Homeless female-headed families: relationships at risk', *Marriage and Family Review*, vol 20, no 1/2, pp 143-59.

Stepney, P., Lynch, R. and Jordan, B. (1999) 'Poverty, exclusion and New Labour', *Critical Social Policy*, vol 19, no 1, pp 109-27.

Straus, M., Gelles, R. and Steinmetz, S. (1980) *Behind closed doors: Violence in the American family*, New York, NY: Doubleday.

Straus, M. and Gelles, R. (1990) *Physical violence in American families: Risk factors and adaptations to violence in 8145 families*, New Brunswick, NJ: Transaction Publishers.

Thams, L. (1999) *Sårbare enlige mødre og deres børn – specielt med henblik på tilknytningen mellem mor og barn* [*Vulnerable lone mothers and their children – with special focus on attachment between mother and child*], Afhandling, København: Danmarks Lærerhøjskole.

Tomkins, A., Mohamed, S., Steinman, M., Macolini, R., Kenning, M. and Afrank, J. (1994) 'The plight of children who witness woman battering: psychological knowledge and policy implications', *Law and Psychology Review*, vol 18, Spring, pp 137-87.

Toner, R. (1995) 'Senate passes bill to abolish guarantees of aid for the poor', *The New York Times*, 20 September.

US Census Bureau (2000a) 'Detailed Poverty Tables', *Current population survey March 2000*, Table 1, P60 Package, Washington, DC: US Government Printing Office.

US Census Bureau (2000b) 'Poverty in the United States', *Current population reports*, Series P60-210, Washington, DC: US Government Printing Office.

US General Accounting Office (1993) *Review of health and safety standards at child care facilities*, Washington, DC: Department of Health and Human Services.

US Senate Judiciary Committee (1990) 'Women and violence hearings', *Senate Hearing*, 101-939, pts 2 and 79, 29 August and 11 December.

Välfärdsprojektet (1996) *Ensamföräldrarna – en utsatt grupp?* [*Lone parents – a vulnerable group?*], Stockholm: Välfärdsprojektet, Skriftserien Nr 2.

Walker, L. (1979) *The battered woman*, New York, NY: Harper and Row.

Walker, L. (1984) *The battered woman syndrome*, New York, NY: Springer Publishing Co.

Walker, L. (1989) 'Psychology and violence against women', *American Psychologist*, vol 44, no 4, pp 695-702.

Appendix A-1: Lone mother research profile

Name	Age	Number of children	Number of interview mothers	Date of interview with mothers	Interview with pedagogue and/or teacher	Date of interview with pedagogue/ teacher
Ditte	23	1	3	summer 96 fall 96 summer 97	pedagogue	fall 96
Lone	26	3	3	summer 96 fall 96 summer 97	teacher	fall 97
Linda	30	1	3	summer 96 fall 96 summer 97	pedagogue	fall 97
Sanne	29	2	3	summer 96 fall 96 summer 97	pedagogue	fall 97
Gina	28	2	3	summer 96 fall 96 summer 97	pedagogue and teacher	fall 97
Jette	26	1	3	summer 96 fall 96 summer 97	pedagogue	fall 97

Appendix A-1: Lone mother research profile cntd.../

Name	Age	Number of children	Number of interview mothers	Date of interview with mothers	Interview with pedagogue and/or teacher	Date of interview with pedagogue/ teacher
Maria	26	1	3	summer 96 fall 96 summer 97	pedagogue	fall 97
Hanne	35	2	3	summer 96 fall 96 summer 97	pedagogue and teacher	fall 97 fall 97
Mona	39	1	2	summer 96 fall 97	–	–
Zeinab	26	1	3	summer 96 fall 96 fall 97	–	–
Adriana	30	2	1	summer 96	–	–
Carmina	30	3	1	summer 96	–	–
Deborah	25	1	1	summer 96	–	–
Emilie	37	2	1	summer 96	–	–

Appendix A-2: Lone mother life obstacles

Name	Level of education	Source of income	Labour market	Network of family/friends	Health conditions	Domestic violence
Ditte	10th grade	SU*	unemployed and pursuing education	weak	depression	no
Lone	10th grade	social assistance	unemployed	weak	depression	yes
Linda	3 years of training (shop assistant)	unemployment benefits + part-time wages	part-time job (clerical)	weak	panic, anxiety	no
Sanne	HF⁺	social assistance	unemployed	weak	depression, pneumonia, PTSD	yes
Gina	10th grade	social assistance	unemployed	weak	depression	yes
Jette	HF	unemployment compensation	educational training (nursing)	some	depression	no
Maria	HF	§43 (rehabilitation assistance)	educational training (pedagogy)	weak	depression	no
Hanne	8th grade	wages	working (hospital cafeteria)	weak	stress-related health problems	yes
Mona	HF	§43 (rehabilitation assistance)	educational training (pedagogy)	some	none	no

Appendix A-2: Lone mother life obstacles cntd.../

Name	Level of education	Source of income	Labour market	Network of family/friends	Health conditions	Domestic violence
Zeinab	one year of HF	social assistance	unemployed	weak	depression	yes
Adriana	completed basic requirements in native country	§43 (rehabilitation assistance)	currently in High School	weak	back problems	yes
Carmina	home help assistant	social assistance	unemployed	weak	anxiety	yes
Deborah	Bachelor's degree in native country	social assistance	unemployed	weak	none	no
Emilie	clerical assistant	social assistance	unemployed	weak	allergies, eczema, nausea	yes

Notes: * SU (see Chapter 2, Note 1)
+ HF (see Chapter 3, Note 4)

Appendix A-3: Child profile

Mother/child	Age	Gender	Health problems	Witnessed/been subjected to violence from father	Contact with father	Witnessed/been subjected to violence from mother's partner
Ditte/Julia	5 months	F	none	no	very infrequent	no
Lone/Peter	3 months	M	none	no	none	no
Lone/Michelle	3 years	F	none	maybe	very infrequent	no
Lone/Jesper	6 years	M	PTSD, deep anxiety	yes	infrequent	no
Linda/Nikolaj	4 years	M	eye problems/ear infections	no	yes	no
Sanne/Michael	1 year	M	none	yes	yes	no
Sanne/Kasper	4 years	M	PTSD, insecure and hyperactive	yes	very infrequent	yes
Gina/Gabriella	2 years	F	bronchial problems	maybe	yes	no
Gina/Jon	9 years	M	ADHD	yes	very infrequent	yes
Jette/Morten	4 years	M	eye problems	no	no (father dead)	no
Maria/Diego	3 years	M	hyperactive	no	no	no
Hanne/Mark	13 years	M	stomach problems	yes	yes	no

Appendix A-3: Child profile cntd.../

Mother/child	Age	Gender	Health problems	Witnessed/been subjected to violence from father	Contact with father	Witnessed/been subjected to violence from mother's partner
Hanne/Søren	6 years	M	dental problems, asthma, eczema, bed wetting	no	yes	no
Mona/Dennis	10 years	M	ear infections, eczema, asthmatic bronchitis and bed wetting	no	yes	no
Zeinab/Yasser	10 years	M	anxiety	yes	yes	no
Carmina/1st child	4 years	M	anxiety	yes	yes	no
Carmina/2nd child	3 years	M	anxiety	yes	yes	no
Carmina/3rd child	2 years	F	anxiety	yes	yes	no
Deborah/Sarah	18 months	F	none	no	yes	no
Emilie/Maja	6 years	F	anxiety	yes	yes	no
Emilie/Pania	2 years	F	anxiety	yes	yes	no
Adriana/Carl	10 years	M	none	yes	yes	no
Adriana/Anna	2 years	F	none	maybe	yes	no

Appendix B: Overview of the income levels of various public sources of support for single mothers with one child

The currency equivalents for the dollar, pound and Danish krone (Dkr) (February 2001) are: $1 = £0.6865 = 8.1260 Dkr

Rates per month as of 1 July 2000

1) Gross Cash Benefit (under the Act on Active Social Policy)	9.865 DKr
2) Rehabilitation* (support of social education under the Act on Active Social Policy)	12.350 DKr
3) Highest unemployment benefit+ (under Law of unemployment insurance)	12.350 DKr
4) SU grant/student loan for those over 20• (under Act on State Education Grant and Loan Scheme)	
Grant	3.907 DKr
Student Loan	2.031 DKr

All amounts are subject to tax, with the exception of the student loan.

Rates per quarter for the child (up to 18 years of age)

Ordinary Child Benefit	923 DKr
Extra Child Benefit	939 DKr
Child-family Grant:	
0-2 years old	2.925 DKr
3-6 years old	2.650 DKr
7-17 years old	2.100 DKr
Minimum Advance Child Maintenance support (non-custodial parent)	887 DKr

Housing subsidy

If applicable, housing subsidy is calculated from the income, number of children together with the size and rent of the house.

*Formerly §43 under the former Act on Social Assistance (1976); now §46 under the Act on Active Social Policy. No 1087 of 13/12-2000.

+ No 1253 of 20/12-2000.

• No 558 of 31/7-1998.

Index

Printed and bound by CPI Group (UK) Ltd, Croydon, CR0 4YY

13/04/2025

14656589-0004